Glasgow
Queen Street

A Railway Station
Renaissance

Ann Glen

Contents

The publishers and Network Rail acknowledge the following for their assistance and support to
to this publication:

Balfour Beatty
Dem-Master Demolition Ltd
J&D Pierce Ltd
Story Contracting

Published by
Lily Publicaions Ltd
PO Box 33, Ramsey, Isle of Man, British Isles IM99 4LP
Tel: 01624 898446
www.lilypublications.co.uk

Foreword

Since first opening its doors in 1842, Queen Street station has been serving the city and people of Glasgow for nearly 180 years.

The station, like the city around it, has changed considerably over the intervening years – evolving to meet the needs of both the railway's growth and Glasgow's prosperity.

The most dramatic change took place in 1878 when the station received its distinctive barrel roof that continues to span the main platforms today.It's fair to say that not all of its 178 years have been kind to Queen Street – with the station being slowly enclosed behind office blocks and hotel extensions.

By the 1970s, with the station almost completely hidden from view, it would have been easy for a visitor to have walked through George Square without even knowing Queen Street was there.

Thankfully, that is something we are now putting right – creating a landmark new façade which brings Queen Street out into the heart of the city centre it serves.

Over the last three years, our engineers and contractors have been working around-the-clock to create an iconic new station, in a £120m transformation which has been successfully delivered without closing Queen Street to its passengers. And that has been no easy task.

The third busiest station on our network, Queen Street handles around 20 million passengers a year and serves as the gateway to Dundee, Inverness, Aberdeen and the West Highlands.

The station is also the main hub for travel between Glasgow and Edinburgh and for commuters, students and shoppers travelling into the city from across the Central Belt.

Work on the redevelopment began in earnest in late 2017 when our engineers began to demolish the 1970s buildings in front of the Victorian station to clear the space for the new expanded concourse.

Over the course of a year, more than 14,000 tons of material had to be removed from the site as mini-diggers were used to demolish the buildings piece by piece from the top down.

Over 94 percent of the resulting demolition material was recycled – with some of it even returning to the station to be used as aggregate in the foundations of the new concourse.

In December 2018 the steel frame of the new station began to go up and the station

truly took on its distinctive new shape in September 2019 when the last of the 310 glass panels on the new frontage was installed.

Inside, the changes have been no less dramatic, with the old travel centre and staff accommodation block on Dundas Street having given way to an extended platform 1.

Platforms 2, 3, 4 and 5 have all been extended to accommodate our new longer electric trains as the station helps to play its part in making rail the greenest form of public travel available to Scots.

The redeveloped station now boasts a larger concourse than before with double the circulation space for the growing number of passengers expected to use Queen Street in the years ahead.

The facilities for our customers have also been greatly improved, with a new travel centre, toilets and shop units. The station is also now fully accessible with lifts into the new building from Queen Street and step-free access from Dundas and North Hanover Streets.

In many ways the rejuvenated Queen Street is a symbol of Scotland's Railway as a whole – proud of its past but designed for the future and with the needs of customers at the heart of everything it does.

Alex Hynes,
Managing Director of Scotland's Railway

Right: *The Victorian train shed at Queen Street station with its barrel-vaulted roof was completed in 1881and is now unique in Scotland.*

Introduction

Queen Street station is a remarkable survivor from the beginnings of the Railway Age. Here Scotland's first intercity route, the Edinburgh & Glasgow Railway, opened in February 1842, and passengers have been joining or arriving on trains at Queen Street ever since. The station has experienced transformations, notably in the 1870s when its Victorian train shed was constructed. It continues to make the best use of a constricted site in a former sandstone quarry – a site that could be got relatively cheaply albeit at the foot of a steep incline.

Queen Street station has kept open in peace and war, and retains its place as a transport hub of the first importance in Glasgow. As a city terminus, it has hitherto been largely hidden from view by other buildings, having only a shy presence for a facility of such significance in a near city centre location.

How has Queen Street escaped plundering hands? After the Second World War, radical reconstruction was proposed for Glasgow's Inner City. The Bruce Report of 1945, had it been implemented, would have caused utter devastation in Central Glasgow, including the loss of its four railway termini – to be replaced by 'North' and 'South' stations on either side of the Clyde. Queen Street station would have been relegated to bus station use. This brutal plan was set aside, its immense cost was insupportable and the city would have lost its Victorian character that is now better appreciated.

In 1951 came the Inglis Report with proposals for integrated road and rail transport in the Glasgow region. The committee faced censure as it had no representative from Glasgow Corporation, although the Corporation was responsible for a major transport network – its famous Glasgow trams. What was a positive outcome from Inglis was the intention to electrify the city's suburban railways.

Then came the Beeching recommendations of 1963 that were contained in the report 'The Re-shaping of British Railways'. This was

Queen Street station's setting in Glasgow's city centre is revealed when looking south over the platform ends when lengthening was in progress   – the City Chambers is on the left.

aimed at improving the railways' financial position, and its proposals radically altered the rail network. Compared with other parts of Britain where the 'Beeching Axe' was swung, Central Scotland got off lightly – said to be on socio-economic grounds. However, the report left Glasgow with only two terminal stations, Central and Queen Street. It was believed that the recent investment in the electrification of the Low Level system, completed in 1960, saved Queen Street – although a generous site for a major new station was available at Buchanan Street.

By this stage, much of the railway's architecture was seen as old fashioned, soot-stained and outmoded. However opinions about ' railway heritage' were becoming polarised, especially following the demolition of the Doric Propylaeum at Euston Station and its listed Great Hall in 1960. Official apathy only fuelled a determination to protect and save what was left, and the influential Victorian Society was set up in London, matched by conservation groups in other cities – but changing opinions took time.

With ignorance about the aesthetic value of heritage buildings widespread, for railway stations the issue was largely about money. Budgets were rarely adequate to permit proper conservation – often a coat of paint and new signage had to do the trick. However, in the 1970s, Queen Street got a glossy new Travel Centre with offices for staff above when the masonry arches on Dundas Street were removed. Soon the classical former Wardlaw church followed and the steel-framed buildings of Consort House and a hotel extension appeared. Architecturally, both were banal at a time when commercial design and railway architecture reached a nadir and neither gave any real enhancement to the station or to the city.

It has taken time to climb out of the trough of such depressing standards, but by the 1990s a new architectural vogue was appearing – initially for cultural venues. Described as 'deconstructivism', its proponents were *avant garde* architects who led the way with some expensive and exotic buildings that caught public attention. It has taken about thirty years for such trend-setting structures to have a 'spin off' in the every day cityscape, but 'deconstructive' elements have percolated into the architectural mainstream where makers of components, such as gold-plated panels or wafer-thin stonework, can offer these at attainable prices.

From a design perspective, odd shapes such as triangles and surfaces that are not

A refurbished milepost from the Edinburgh & Glasgow Railway, opened at Queen Street in February 1842, is again in view on the concourse. John McLaughlin

rectilinear can now be achieved with 'autocad' programmes. What might have begun on the back of an envelope, with computer modelling can be drafted in 3D down to the last millimetre the following day.

Such influences have fed into the solutions now seen at Queen Street station. It has gained a well-lit southern façade, a spacious concourse and long platforms. Its new basement houses facilities that are 'top of the range' and fully accessible. As a terminus station, at last it is visible, enhancing the passenger experience with daylight at its platforms as a blessing, while making a positive statement about railways in Glasgow's cityscape.

Queen Street station has a footfall in the order of 19 million a year – reflecting an increase of some 30 per cent in passenger numbers on ScotRail services in 10 years. What do forecasts say? On the E&G route alone, passenger numbers are projected to grow by a further 40 per cent. If such increases are to be sustained, how will a station like Queen Street cope? Given the likely significance of 'low emission' rail transport on passenger numbers, will additional station capacity have to be developed at some stage, such as a revived St Enoch or super Buchanan Street? Meantime, Queen Street is Scotland's third busiest station and only now – from a passenger perspective – is it looking up to the task.

Ann Glen, MBE FRSGS

Chapter 1

Queen Street Station begins

The first railway terminus in Glasgow was at Townhead, on high ground to the north of the small but growing city on the banks of the Clyde. The Townhead terminus was in Glebe Street, by St Rollox, close to the 'Cut of Junction' between the Monkland Canal and the Forth & Clyde Canal. The Garnkirk & Glasgow Railway came here in 1831 – a line constructed from Lanarkshire westwards to outdo its near neighbour the Monkland Canal in carrying coal to Glasgow. From the outset the G&GR promoters had determined to run it in direct opposition to the canal that was reputed to overcharge. The Tennant brothers, whose extensive chemical works stood beside the canal basin at Townhead, were the leading sponsors of the G&GR – they required large quantities of coal on a regular basis for the production of chlorine bleach for the textile industry, and rail transit was the answer. The new line was soon competing for traffic effectively, as being 'managed and operated as a railway in its own right', it offered regular goods and passenger services, both steam and horse-hauled. It not only saved the slow miles of canal transit but also the dues and charges thereon.

From Townhead, the G&GR ran east for just over 8 miles to meet the Monkland & Kirkintilloch Railway at Gartsherrie – a place then in countryside near modern day Coatbridge. The M&KR was a coal railway authorised in 1824 – and it was the first line anywhere to specify the use of steam locomotives in its Act. Both railways used the Scotch gauge of 4ft 6in that was typical at the time. The M&KR was also a deliberate move to outflank the Monkland Canal and defeat its monopoly of the coal trade. This it achieved by taking consignments to the Forth & Clyde Canal at Kirkintilloch from where the loads could be shipped to either Glasgow or Edinburgh.

The G&GR scored in giving an all rail route from the Monklands rich coalfield to Glasgow. The engineers were Thomas Grainger and John Miller who had established a partnership in 1825. Grainger was the senior partner, whose birthplace in 1794 was Gogar Green west of Edinburgh. He became a prominent civil engineer specialising in railways. John Miller was born in Ayr in 1805, the son of a wright and builder. He was a student at Edinburgh University before forsaking law for mathematics and training in land surveying. Grainger and Miller became partners and from the 1830s they led numerous projects in Central Scotland and further a-field. One was the Dundee & Arbroath Railway of 1838, for which Miller took greater responsibility, but their partnership ceased in 1847. Miller's outstanding initial achievement

The opening of the Garnkirk & Glasgow Railway on 27 September 1831 was a ceremonial event that saw Stephenson 2-2-0 'Planet' locomotives hauling trains at Townhead near St Rollox chemical works. (After D.O. Hill)

would be the Edinburgh & Glasgow Railway opened in February 1842. By 1850 when he retired from practice, he was a wealthy man who had built more railways in Scotland than any other engineer, including the line to Ayr and via Kilmarnock to Carlisle – most of the routes now continuing in daily use as part of the Scottish network.

For the G&GR, Grainger and Miller would show their capabilities in producing a line that was as far as possible 'straight and level', or at least with gradients that were relatively gentle. This required earthmoving on a substantial scale – impressive features were the long cutting at Provanmill and the massive embankment at Germiston. Although the 'Scotch gauge' of 4ft 6in was chosen, it was a double track system and has been described as Scotland's first 'proper railway'. George Stephenson's 'Planet' locomotives could run on it at speed. At the ceremonial opening on 27 September 1831, an event recorded by the artist David Octavius Hill, both passenger and goods trains were demonstrated to crowds by the line sides with Grainger and Miller on the footplates of the locomotives. There was a banquet in the Black Bull Inn at the Trongate where the Lord Provost ventured the hope that there would soon be a railway between Glasgow and Edinburgh.

The site at Townhead was primarily a coal depot, being arranged for handling such traffic; a view by Hill shows loading structures to supply carts for local sales, and facilities to transfer coal to barges on the Forth & Clyde Canal system. Glasgow's city centre was then at the Trongate in Argyle Street, which was the transport hub for stage coach traffic, both local and long distance, and accessing the G&GR from there was not easy. The choice was either a lengthy walk up the High Street to reach Glebe Street, the nearest place of note to the Townhead, or to book a seat on a coach. For such a transit, a tollgate belonging to the Inchbelly Road Trust on Parliamentary Road was an obstacle where a charge had to be paid, but avoiding this inconvenience involved a long detour. Inevitably, this barrier led to disputes and a Court of Session case, the first wrangle over a station in the city.

Facilities for passengers on the G&GR at Townhead were rudimentary. Only a small booking office and 'passenger hall', just a modest waiting room, had been constructed. The advice contained in an issue of 'The Railway Times', had warned railway companies against 'squandering the funds of the constituents on ostentatious buildings', and this appears to have been followed. Premises were also built 'for the attention to locomotives' – the phrase 'engine shed' had not yet been coined.

After opening, the G&GR soon had trains of

The engine shed, with a flat above, on the G&GR at its Glebe Street depot, Townhead, Glasgow in the 1960s. (Postcard & Covers)

26 to 28 wagons laden with coal, fireclay, stone and other freight in action, justifying the outlays in cuttings and embankments to make the haulage of such heavy loads possible. The usual speed was 10 to 12mph, though a train with 16 empties and a carriage with nine passengers was said to have reached over 40mph.

To counteract the G&GR's unsatisfactory location on the town's outskirts, the company set about promoting the line for passengers. Note may have been taken of the success of the Edinburgh & Dalkeith Railway in attracting people to take jaunts out of the capital into the Lothian countryside. So the G&GR advertised 'a pleasant, healthful and cheap excursion of about 16 miles to and from the country', a round trip that took some 2 hours. This let passengers satisfy their curiosity about rail travel and feel the thrill of speed. So popular was the jaunt that during Glasgow Fair Week in July 1832, seven trains had to be run each way daily instead of the usual four. This rural 'whirl' was even more attractive for family parties when the G&GR built 'a commodious inn' at Gartsherrie, offering 'every convenience'. It is claimed that Gartsherrie

An office of the G&GR at Townhead beside a railway crossing that also reveals a turnplate (with a wooden cover) where two lines met. (Glasgow Life)

The Townhead depot of the G&GR where coal from the Monklands district was brought for distribution in rivalry with the Monkland Canal. (After D.O.Hill)

A timetable for the G&GR for its summer services in the 1830s. (Gartcoshlocalhistory)

Inn was the first railway refreshment room in the world. The stone structure was latterly a station with housing for staff, but was removed in the 1960s before its historical significance was appreciated.

For the early lines, there was much to be learned about running a railway. For instance, the G&GR only set up its booking office in March 1837, 'adopting the plan of supplying passengers with tickets before starting'. Then there was the matter of stations – intermediate stops had yet to have raised platforms, a booking office and

waiting rooms, but even without any facilities at all such stops were considered 'stations'. Passengers might step down into mud by the line at a journey's end.

When the G&GR reached Gartsherrie and met the Monkland & Kirkintilloch Railway, the latter refused to allow its engines onto the M&KR line – horse-haulage had to be used to reach Leaend near Airdrie. This was frustrating for the G&GR as it was designed for the use of steam engines – their 'facility and velocity' clearly demonstrated the supremacy of locomotives. Thanks to the G&GR, Airdrie coal could now reach Glasgow at one-third of the cost of horse haulage plus a Monkland Canal transit.

After the Liverpool & Manchester line opened in 1830 and soon proved very profitable, there was a growing enthusiasm for railways. A railway connecting Scotland's two major cities Edinburgh and Glasgow became an enticing proposition. However, an attempt in 1831 by Grainger and Miller to use the Garnkirk & Glasgow line as the initial element in an intercity route was refused by Parliament.

In 1835 the Slamannan Railway, crossing the peaty uplands of Central Scotland where minerals might lie beneath, obtained its Act and it opened in 1838. Its directors saw the possibility of making a linkage between the two cities, using four railways and a canal. Intrepid travellers would begin at Glasgow on the G&GR, join the M&KR near Airdrie, then transfer to the Ballochney Railway. This line was just 5 miles long with steep inclines varying from 1 in 22 to 1in 25; on these, self-acting inclined planes with hemp ropes had been installed. Laden wagons coming downhill took the empties – with a vehicle to carry passengers – back up. Working expenses were therefore low. Transferring to the

Gartsherrie station near Coatbridge was originally an inn popular with excursionists on the G&G; it was the earliest railway refreshment room in Britain but the building was removed in the 1950s. (Airdrie Library)

Slamannan Railway would lead to Causewayend – the journey to Edinburgh being completed by swift boat on the Union Canal or by coach. It was claimed that passengers could go out and back between the cities in a day.

Meantime a rash of railway promotions on the south bank of the Clyde had caught public attention. In 1835, the Paisley & Renfrew Railway was authorised, a short line to form a link to a steamboat wharf on the Clyde. This was followed by an Act in 1837 for the Glasgow, Paisley & Greenock Railway, a route designed by the eminent engineer, Joseph Locke. He had a hand in the Grand Junction Railway linking Birmingham and Liverpool, but achieved fame with the Lancaster & Preston Railway of 1840, followed by the line over Shap to Carlisle. With Thomas Errington, he would also be responsible for the Caledonian Railway from Carlisle over Beattock summit into the Clyde Valley and thus to Glasgow.

The Glasgow, Paisley, Kilmarnock and Ayr Railway was progressing under John Miller's direction. Between Glasgow and Paisley lines would be shared with the Greenock line and in July 1840, the Glasgow & Paisley Joint Railway opened. Accommodation was provided for both companies initially at a temporary station at Bridge Street close to the Broomielaw. The latter was a key departure point for steamship services to the Scottish coast and islands, to Ireland and to Liverpool. From the perspective of sea links, the position was well chosen but the north bank of the Clyde would win out as it had in the past – with the cathedral, university and markets being sited there, ensuring that it would be the effective centre of the city.

By April 1841, a permanent Bridge Street

The first proper station in Glasgow was Bridge Street on the Clyde's south bank. Opened in 1840, it served both the Glasgow, Paisley, Kilmarnock & Ayr and the Glasgow, Paisley and Greenock Railways. (wikipedia)

station had opened – the first proper station in Glasgow. Designed by architect James Collie from Aberdeen, it was a handsome structure in classical style with a portico of Doric columns. It had a remarkable 'porte cochère' that led to the interior 25ft (8m) above street level – and passengers had to ascend stairs, causing some citizens to be puzzled as to how the locomotives and trains for opening day had been got into the station. The two companies had separate booking offices, but the station's layout with just two short platforms and five lines had been arranged by John Miller.

At the third attempt, the Edinburgh & Glasgow Railway won its Act on 4 July 1838. Its determined promoter, John Leadbetter, a successful Glasgow linen merchant, would become company chairman. He now looked for a site for a terminus station for the E&G, as it would become known. He was an active citizen, taking part in many enterprises for the benefit of the city and its people – he served on the Town Council, the Merchants' House and the Trades'

To gain rail access to Bridge Street station, elaborate skew bridges were required, such as this structure at Cooke Street. (S J Brees, Railway Practice 1839)

Top left: A view from the southeast of George Square, Glasgow, shows the town houses on its north side in this sketch by Joseph Swan in 1829. (wikipedia)

Top right: John Leadbetter, advocate for railways and chairman of the Edinburgh & Glasgow Railway Company from 1835 to 1842. (Mitchell Library, Glasgow)

House, and in addition he supported the improvement of navigation on the Clyde and the advance of technical education.

A possible site came to Leadbetter's attention northwest of the town centre and close to the residential district of George Square. This had developed on two acres of land belonging to the Ramshorn Croft on a site bought in the 1770s by the Town Council of Glasgow from Hutchesons' Hospital, a charitable organisation dating from the 17th century. By 1778 with building in progress nearby – in what is now the Merchant City – the ground had become a dumping ground for soil and waste. Sheep could be grazed there, but it was poorly drained. In 1825 the Corporation engaged the curator of the town's Royal Botanic Gardens, then at Sandyford, to improve it. Trees and shrubs were planted, winding walks were made, and the new garden area was enclosed with railings. As an expression of loyalty, George Square was named after King George III, although his statue was omitted. The loss of the American colonies after 1783 had angered the city's Tobacco Lords by spoiling their lucrative trade. However, a dutiful supporter of the monarchy had earlier renamed Cow Loan as 'Queen Street', after Queen

Charlotte, the King's consort.

With Glasgow expanding, in 1792 the Town Council – perhaps inspired by Craig's design for the New Town of Edinburgh – approved a grid plan for the city with streets set out at right angles from Glassford Street west to Buchanan Street. This would continue going west over the hill on the Blythswood estate. By the 1820s, George Square had become a desirable residential area lined with terraced town houses of three storeys – sketches show a touch of domesticity with washing poles on the green. The grandest tribute would be to Sir Walter Scott, taking the form of a Doric column with his statue on top, a monument that was erected in 1837.

Leadbetter's preferred site for a station was on land that was formerly the site of Bailie Crauford's mansion, and long ago had been farmed in 'runrig'. Although trees still grew there and rooks nested, it was a place likely to be overwhelmed by the expanding town. On the west side was the St Enoch Burn (now in a sewer) and close by, sandstone quarries had been opened to produce blond stone for the buildings taking shape westwards. The quarries were known as Cracklinghouse, Dowanside and Ewing's, and they resulted in terrain with deep excavations.

Through Leadbetter's trade as a linen merchant, he had useful contacts – one was with James Ewing, a fellow magistrate and owner of the afore-mentioned quarry. Ewing was wealthy, influential and a former Lord Provost, who had purchased the old feu of Bailie Crauford's mansion, probably as a speculation. On 2 March 1837, through Leadbetter's foresight, negotiations were begun on behalf of the

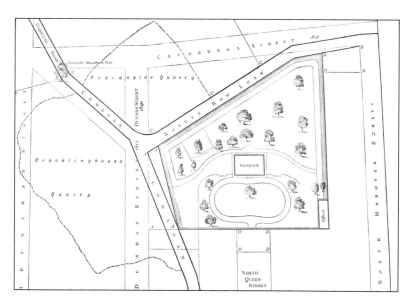

The site for Queen Street station was on the former feu of Bailie Crauford's mansion and close to quarries. (Regality Papers, Glasgow City Archives)

E&GR and at Whitsun 1838, he purchased the feu – just a triangle of land at Dundas Street of about 3½ acres in extent. A stance was also bought in North Hanover Street. A former quarry might be thought an undesirable site for a station but the land could be got cheaply - and it would give the E&GR terminus an enviable central location at low cost, while the North Hanover Street stance would subsequently make a goods yard.

For James Ewing, the railway development was an opportunity to dispose of an awkward site. Indeed, the arrival of the railways altered the supply chains for building stone completely – quarries no longer had to be close to construction sites or near water transport. From now on, stone could be chosen for its appearance and quality rather than for its convenient location – and soon hauled by rail from any distance.

In the spring of 1838, with the Bill for the Edinburgh & Glasgow Railway before a House of Lords Committee, John Miller, now appointed the engineer for the project, appeared. His answers were revealing:–

Q. *Is the line before Parliament the best line between Glasgow and Edinburgh?*

JM. *I have no doubt of it. It would be a line with a ruling gradient of 1 in 880 ...to all appearance as flat as that table.*

To achieve such a gradient would call for prodigious effort – with long cuttings in rock, impressive viaducts across deep valleys, and tunnels at Winchburgh, Falkirk and Glasgow. The gentle profile would allow early steam

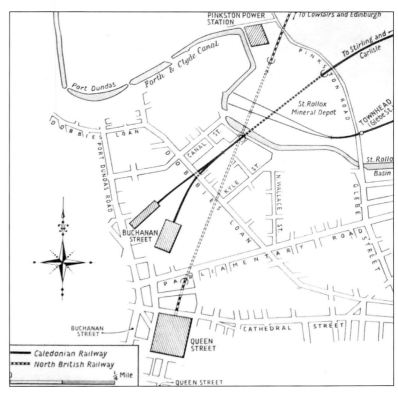

locomotives to be used successfully and high speeds would be attainable. Although Miller had knowledge of the geology on the route – the first geological map of Scotland had been published in 1835 – he had engaged a team to make borings down to 100 to 150 feet (30 to 45m) from one end of the route to the other, an investigation that had taken several months.

The approach to Glasgow would be especially challenging. After substantial cuttings at

A map showing the proposed alignment of the Edinburgh & Glasgow Railway from Queen Street and the subsequent line of the Caledonian Railway from Buchanan Street, with the 'pinch point' where both went below the Port Dundas branch of the Forth & Clyde Canal. (Railway Magazine)

The Queen Street station site was compromised by old quarries, Cracklinghouse, Dovanside and Ewing's quarries. (Glasgow Forum)

James Ewing of Strathleven who sold the site for Queen Street station to the Edinburgh & Glasgow Railway Company in 1838. (The Merchants' House of Glasgow)

Bishopbriggs and Colston, from Cowlairs the tracks would have to descend to city level near George Street. On the way, the railway would have to negotiate a strategic location – below the Cut of Junction of the Port Dundas branch of the Forth & Clyde Canal with the Monkland Canal. With the rails being 69ft (21.15m) below the Cut of Junction, it would keep the lines clear of canal activity at Port Dundas. The original intention was to have placed a station near that harbour but canal opposition prevented this. An overbridge or viaduct was also considered and rejected.

The steep descent into the city would be at 1 in 42 for1¼ miles (2km).

Miller was questioned at length about this steep approach to Glasgow.

Q. *How many tunnels?* JM. *Three*. These would vary in length, with deep cuttings in sandstone and mudstone between each, the longest at 330yds (301m) being under the canal. The openings would serve as 'smoke vents' to clear the air and improve visibility. The tunnels would be 28ft (8.6m) wide but only 18ft high (5.4m). This was lower than the proposal for the tunnel at Falkirk.

The Cowlairs tunnel section showing the gradient profile from Queen Street station where most of the ascent is at 1 in 41. (Railway Magazine)

Q. *Why lower?* JM. *There are no Locomotive Engines to go through and they are double the height of carriages.*

Surprisingly, Miller was not asked about the inclined plane installation that would require a stationary steam engine to be positioned at the summit at Cowlairs.

The terminus for the E&GR would thus be located at the north end of Queen Street where access by rail would be awkward. An abandoned quarry site was basically derelict land with stone waste, and Miller explained how this would be treated. *'We shall open it, cut it and build over again – it is what we call 'cut and cover'.*

However, the site had advantages – it was close to the Royal Exchange, a business hub for the city.

Q. *Is the termination in Glasgow an exceedingly favourable termination?*

JM. *Very much so. It is at George Square – only about 1,000 yards (914m) from the proposed Depot of the Ayrshire and Greenock. The Railways will unite there.*

Miller did not mention that that the Ayrshire & Greenock terminus would be at Bridge Street on the *south* side of the Clyde, but he was right to emphasise the E&GR station's 'near city centre' choice as advantageous. John Leadbetter's shrewd negotiation for land close to Dundas Street at a bargain price would give the E&GR a flying start in Glasgow.

Although inclined planes at city termini were used on some early railways, such as on the London & Birmingham Railway at Camden in its pre-Euston years, there were concerns about the inclined plane and its safe working. Miller explained that the approach to Glasgow would end in ' a small piece on the level' and the station site would also have to accommodate a tunnel mouth. What had been Rottenrow Loan was soon transformed by the presence of the railway into Cathedral Street where an elaborate bridge would incorporate the tunnel mouth. The railway soon changed the character of the whole district.

The House of Lords Committee asked further

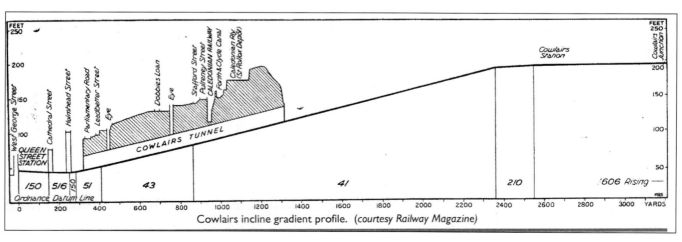

Cowlairs incline gradient profile. (*courtesy Railway Magazine*)

questions about passenger safety relating to the incline:–

Q. *The danger is in going down?* JM. *Much the same when you are hanging on the End of a Rope, It does not signify much whether you are going down or up.*

Q. *If it were to give way?* JM. *The Waggons would go down.* Q. *And the Passengers in them?* JM. *Yes.*

At that time, the Edinburgh & Dalkeith Railway, a horse-drawn waggonway, built essentially for coal haulage, had a tunnel at 1 in 30. It was carrying up to 200,000 passengers a year in converted stagecoaches on pleasure jaunts into Lothian countryside. Miller did not consider the gradient dangerous when vehicles were 'perfectly under the control of the Breaks' (sic).

Q. *If not applied in time, the Result could be fearful?* JM. *Yes, it would be dreadful, no Doubt; 1 in 40 is perfectly safe using a Fixed Engine.*

Although the site for the proposed station was near George Street and George Square with an opening close to the north end of Queen Street, the frontage was unimpressive. There were two and three storey properties there, but only one building of distinction that stood on the corner of Dundas Street. This was Dr Wardlaw's Chapel, a classical 'temple' constructed in sandstone for a growing membership of Congregationalists that had moved from modest accommodation in Albion Street in the old Merchant City. The chapel had been designed by James Gillespie Graham, an Edinburgh architect, and opened in 1819. Dr Ralph Wardlaw (1779-1853) was a charismatic preacher who campaigned against slavery and had a large following. By 1842, the E&GR directors already had their eye on this valuable property for use as their head office.

In the general cityscape, the outcome was that the E&GR terminus would be largely hidden from view behind the existing properties in George Street and George Square. To give it some status near a prestigious part of the city, a competition for the design of a gateway was proposed, with 'premiums' offered for the two best designs. However, by 1841, with the railway incomplete, though due to open in July that year, there was a recurring shortage of funds. During the E&GR's construction, additional capital had to be authorised by Parliament on three occasions, there were nine calls for money from subscribers, and finally there had to be recourse to loans to cover expenditure. Regarding the gateway, a first prize of £60 was won by a Glasgow team, but the design was considered 'too expensive to be executed' and a letter on 'economy in the construction of stations' was read to the directors. Lack of money for investment to ensure adequate facilities would plague the Glasgow terminus at Queen Street

The Glasgow Royal Lunatic Asylum where the proposed line of the E&GR passed close to its NW wing with protest made about the proposed tunnel and vent. (Sketch by Joseph Swan, 1829)

over the years.

For early railway developments, the actual acquiring of land was not usually expensive as there were often willing vendors. Another factor was the lack of landowner experience in valuing their property. Railway companies were in a strong position as they had powers through their Acts to deviate up to 100yd (91.4m) on either side of their preferred alignment. The result was that there were few claims for compensation over the approach to Glasgow, but there was one of consequence from the directors of the Glasgow Royal Lunatic Asylum. This establishment was housed in a large cruciform building designed by an able architect William

A proposed modification of the Cowlairs tunnel in 1841 with the 'eyes' closed in response to a compensation claim by the asylum's directors. (Glasgow City Archives, Mitchell Library)

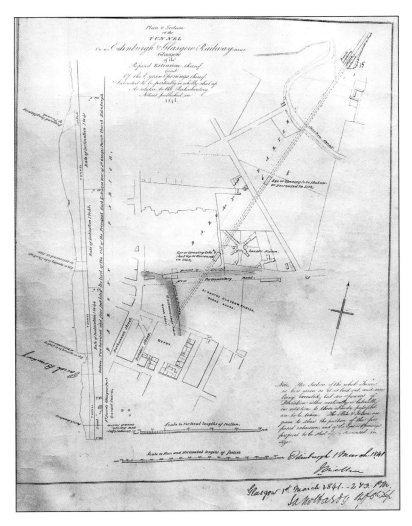

A former tunnel vent at Queen Street with its masonry portal and its concrete 'roof' from where cement was being piped for tunnel works in 2016.

Stark and opened in 1814. Both the structure and grounds lay in close proximity to the alignment of the tunnel and close by would be an 'eye' or opening in the tunnel roof – one of two smoke vents in the structure. The asylum's directors argued that this offensive and polluting 'eye' should be closed and when this failed, they sued for compensation.

If parties could not agree, such a dispute was referred to a jury sitting with a sheriff of the county. Pre-1845 when legislation altered compensation arrangements, landowners came to believe that such juries favoured railways. Experience showed that jurors generally set a sum far less than that claimed, 'frequently less than a quarter', according to a financier. Nevertheless, some claims were plainly ludicrous – the one for £44,000, brought by the asylum's directors over the tunnel and its 'eye' against the E&GR, being in that category. A jury reduced the claim to an award of £873.

With the Act for the E&GR obtained on 4 July 1838, tenders were invited for works on the line. There would be 20 contracts relating to the civil engineering of the railway covering cuttings and embankments, bridges and viaducts. Stations were treated separately and contract 21 was for the Glasgow terminus. In May 1840 there were eight offers to construct the Glasgow station – ranging from £7,211 to £11,885. Miller had contacts with 'a builder of respectability' who would perform 'with spirit and activity'. There would be just two lines at the station – one in, and one out. There were tenders for 'turnplates' – small turntables of 12 or 14ft (3.6 or 4.2m) in diameter. These devices, installed along one side of the station, were essential as carriages and

wagons had to be turned in order that their brakes could be accessed on the same side of a train. The lowest offer of £89 and £109 for these turnplates came from Edington & Son, iron founders in Glasgow.

Though Miller had toyed with a gauge of 5ft 6in (as used on the Dundee & Arbroath line), at an early stage of the E&GR plans, after 'full and deliberate consideration', the gauge of 4ft 8½in was chosen. This was the clear preference for the 'leading English lines now approaching Scotland', and would facilitate integration into a national network and prepare for a high rate of speed. This choice would become 'standard gauge'.

By the summer of 1841, the E&GR should have been completed but an exceptionally wet season had caused rivers and burns to flood and affected cuttings and other new structures. The 'very unfavourable weather' had impeded the contractors and their teams setting work back. There was such a severe delay at Croy Hill, with its mile-long rock cutting in whinstone, that Miller suggested that the line might be opened in two parts – east and west of this obstruction – but the directors held out for total completion.

On Contract 20, extending to 1mile 640yds (2km), the principal work was the tunnel passing under Glasgow. Before a station could be developed, this tunnel had to be formed and the work began in March 1839. There would also be a long open cutting to access the tunnel, and by August 1841, this was 'all but finished'. For the main tunnel, 'guide mines' had been excavated whereby shafts were cut into the rock. From these points, access could be got to excavate horizontally, with spoil being lifted up to the surface for disposal. However, the shafts allowed water to drain into the workings, but there was an answer – by placing stationary steam engines above the shafts and cuttings to pump this out. By the spring of 1840, three steam engines and a horse-gin (a low cost solution) were in action at the Glasgow tunnel, and three distinct portions of the tunnel with its two large 'eyes' were being formed. An impressive tunnel mouth had yet to be constructed – this would be a key feature and the only architectural gesture at the Glasgow terminus. The decision had been taken to lengthen the tunnel's north portion by 50yds (45m) – now making the tunnel 1,099 yd (1004m) long and so taking the line into Glasgow was proving tough. However, track laying was in progress and would take three weeks to complete.

Tenders had been invited for 'Mason-work of the offices and Business Chambers at the Glasgow Station', and with money tight, the lowest offer of £1,273 was accepted, conveniently covering joinery and other works. In June 1840 a scheme to heat the offices with hot water was proposed to the directors – an early venture in central heating – and was considered but not installed. Miller's report in July 1841 noted that the station house and passenger facilities for the Glasgow station were advancing well and progress was also visible at Cowlairs where the engine sheds and workshops were being roofed.

It was not considered practicable to work trains up the tunnel's gradient by relying on the power and adhesion of locomotives alone and a winding engine to operate the inclined plane was required. The engine house, in classical style with its 90ft (27.4m) chimney, was soon reported as complete. The double-beam engine came from Kerr, Neilson & Company, Glasgow, and cost £2,900. An engineer to operate it had been recruited from the Edinburgh & Dalkeith Railway where a stationary steam engine hauled trains up the incline at the St Leonards tunnel. His pay would be 40 shillings a week, plus a house and coals. Trains descending the incline would be controlled by two brakemen each on specially constructed brake wagons.

The purchase of locomotives was now a priority. John Miller led a deputation to the leading English railways 'to enquire into the merits of the different kinds of Engines, Carriages, etc', before contracts were placed for the E&GR. Twenty engines of two types were chosen – from Bury of Manchester and Hawthorn of Newcastle. The choice of passenger carriages covered first, second and third class vehicles; horseboxes, carriage trucks and wagons of various types were also ordered – the quantities being thought sufficient for operating the railway.

The E&GR directors understood the importance of integrated transport and contacts were made with hirers of public coaches that could call at the Glasgow terminus. Posters were soon printed to advertise trains with boards displaying the 'tolls' or fares that passengers would pay to travel on the new railway.

A system of booking and ticketing was discussed as 'Mr Edmondson' had been contacted. Thomas Edmondson, formerly a cabinetmaker, became a stationmaster on the

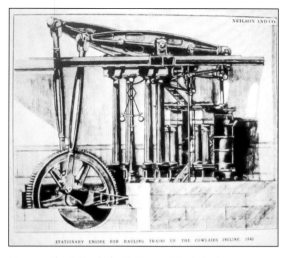

The double-beam engine for the Cowlairs Incline by Kerr, Neilson & Company, Glasgow, cost £2,900. With modifications it continued in use until 1908. (The Engineer, 1922)

Newcastle & Carlisle Railway. His tickets were small cardboard rectangles that could give journey details. They were durable compared with hand written slips of paper and could also carry serial numbers and be date stamped to prevent fraud. To use the 'Edmondson Patent', railway companies had to pay on a mileage basis. Being unable to obtain a reduction in price, the E&GR preferred to have its own paper tickets printed. 'A million and a half' were ordered from McClure & McDonald, the company's Glasgow printers who also handled its advertising, with 200,000 being allocated to the Glasgow terminus alone. John Miller was asked to find a machine to put dates on them, and ticket cases were bought for each station. Reminders were given about having forms for traffic returns, for waybills and for keeping records – for all of which 'Mr Miller's advice' should be taken. So crucial was his expertise seen for the successful running of the railway that he was also to 'give attention for 6 months after the opening of the line'.

Tenders for painting the 'Passenger Shed', a large but simple timber structure, had been issued in October 1841. Shortly, office furniture was ordered for the station. The appointment of staff, such as booking clerks and guards, was begun with 'Mr Miller to advise on suitability' – the Manager of Goods would receive £200 a year but the Superintendent of the Passenger Office at the Glasgow station would receive £120 and

Below right: *A medallion for the Edinburgh & Glasgow Railway's opening shows the imposing tunnel mouth at Cathedral Street that was removed in 1879. (National Railway Museum)*

Below left: *An Edinburgh & Glasgow Railway third class open carriage with seating, a design from 1842. (Allan G Rodgers)*

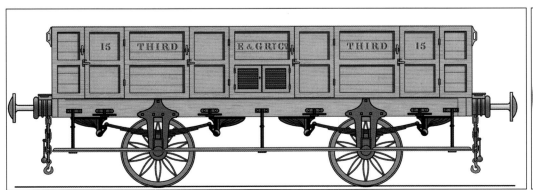

A sketch of an Edinburgh & Glasgow Railway four-wheeled locomotive from Bury of Liverpool as used on the opening day. (S.Everard in NBRSG Journals)

the Superintendent of the station itself only £60 – but he would have a house. The booking clerks for second and third class passengers would each receive £80 but the first class only £70 – it must have been assumed that he would be less busy. The Superintendent of Locomotives would receive £100 a year. E&GR business would be conducted from its Head Office in Glasgow at North Queen Street. Miller recommended that another property should be bought for £2,580 and that there should be insurance against fire for the railway's premises.

In addition, provision was made for 'luggage' or goods traffic; though this would not be promoted initially, it would become a significant element at the Glasgow terminus. A goods shed, with cast iron columns from Robertson & McDougall's foundry at Port Dundas, was therefore constructed on the North Hanover Street side of the new station.

The completion of the line was proving costly, with additional loans underwritten by the directors, but preparations for the opening went ahead. A letter came from the Board of Trade stating that Major-General Pasley would be in Edinburgh on 11 February 1842 and would inspect the railway the following day. This was a repeat visit as General Sir Frederick Smith had viewed the partially finished line in October 1841. The Railway Inspectorate had been set up in 1840, an outcome of the Railway Regulation Act of that year. The 'Inspecting Officers' had military backgrounds – a practice that became a tradition – though they were appointed by the Board of Trade and reported to that government department. Their inspections of new lines were aimed at judging their suitability for passenger trains. A further obligation on the Inspectors would be to investigate any accidents that companies reported and to submit the findings to Parliament.

Only on 14 December 1841 was the purchase of John Leadbetter's site– where Queen Street station would sit – finally agreed for the sum of for £3,150. To reduce the burden on the strained E&GR finances, this was converted to a ground annual of £157 10s with a feu duty of £51 a year – a bargain for such a location in the heart of the city.

The railway was eight months behind schedule when it opened in February 1842. Preparations for the great event advanced with three public viewings arranged for the tunnel at Glasgow and of the one at Falkirk, both being whitewashed and gas-lit – thereby giving reassurance about the safety of such dark holes underground. People could visit the station and walk through the tunnel for a modest charge – at one shilling for gentlemen and 6d for trades' people – the money going to charity. This fund had been set up following the calamitous capsize of a passenger barge on the Paisley Canal. In total, £218 was raised for this charitable purpose.

It had been left to John Miller to arrange the opening ceremony – an unlikely duty for a civil engineer. This would take place at Queen Street, by then commonly referred to as the 'Glasgow station' or 'Dundas Street'. The directors resolved that a train should go from Glasgow to Edinburgh at 'nine o'clock and return at twelve' – and on its return 'an entertainment' should be given in the Passenger Shed 'say at three o'clock'. The train back to Edinburgh would 'start at four o'clock'. However, 'unfavourable weather' delayed the directors' inspection of the line until 31 January, and the grand opening was put back to 18 February 1842. Invitations were sent to civic dignitaries, directors and their friends, to shareholders (with holdings of 'above £100') – in all, to about 1,100 guests.

John Miller obtained four quotations for a 'collation' and the mid-price offer of 7s 6d per head, including champagne and wines, came from the London Hotel in Glasgow, and was accepted. The 'collation' consisted of a selection of cold meats – a light meal 'when there is insufficient time for fuller entertainment' – a wise choice as the two special trains did not run to time on the opening day. An army of waiters served 120 tureens of soups, 400 dishes of potatoes, 30 roast turkeys stuffed with tongue, 40 boiled rounds of beef 'richly glazed and ornamented', 60 dozen lobsters and 600 hundred tartlets. Nothing to match the scale of this banquet had hitherto been seen in Glasgow.

On the opening day, a Glasgow guest wrote, 'By eight o'clock in the morning, hundreds of our citizens were seen wending their way on foot and in carriages towards the Railway Terminus at the head of Queen Street where a strong body of police were stationed to preserve order, and the excellent band of the gallant 10th Foot regaled the ears of the anxious throng'. (This was a Lincolnshire regiment that was forming the Glasgow Garrison at the time).

Guests boarded the carriages from the 'promenades' on either side, and then powered by the stationary engine, the train of carriages was hauled up the tunnel, until they reached

Cowlairs and were ready to be attached to two locomotives. Although *'nine o'clock was the hour of starting, the necessary and multitudinous arrangements delayed the time until twenty-five minutes to ten, when the magnificent convoy of 35 carriages was put in motion by the power of steam, amid the cheers and congratulations of the assembled multitudes'*. Consequently, there was a delayed arrival at Haymarket, and the afternoon was well advanced before the returning passengers, now led by the Edinburgh train with its 30 vehicles and three locomotives, reached the Glasgow terminus. The celebratory meal, though timed for 2.30pm, could only begin at 5pm.

The 'spacious and elegant passenger shed' had been transformed into a banqueting hall, with the rails floored over. Tables were set with 'white calico', the walls draped in pink and white, and the ends covered with crimson drapes arranged in 'Greek style'. Gas lamps were suspended from each colonnade, with temporary pipes installed in the tension rods of the roof where many gas jets were also lit. Behind the top table, there was gas piping in the form of a locomotive, while a circular ornament like a wheel, suitably illuminated, was displayed on the east side.

So large was the hall that trumpeters at either end signalled the call for toasts. The first toast was led by the Lord Provost of Edinburgh, who wished the railway prosperity and success. John Leadbetter, as chairman of the E&GR replied, recalling how in 1832 he had been greatly impressed by the potential of railways after a journey on the Liverpool & Manchester Railway. He then became a staunch supporter of the E&GR scheme. Over three Parliamentary sessions, when journeys to London took four days, it required persistence to counter opposition to the railway from stage coach and canal interests. In 1835 at the commencement of the struggle, the probable cost was put at £550,000, but the project was complex, took longer and was 'much in excess of this', in fact approaching £1.25 million. The 'care and anxious thought' applied to the E&GR had resulted in a railway that was 'the crowning triumph ... a national work that would add greatly to the prosperity of Scotland'. It was now part of a growing railway network that would be 'a monument to Britain's science, enterprise and wealth'. Such was the significance of the opening of the E&GR that a medal was struck in commemoration. There was 'extraordinary interest in the event' and 'the greatest excitement prevailed ... with the public schools on holiday in Glasgow' – even although the tunnels prevented views of the trains.

Champagne was drunk with 'great good humour and heartiness' before it was time for

An opening day ticket shows E&GR trains and major features on the new railway. (Michael Stewart)

the Edinburgh train to set off about 6pm. There was then a delay of some three hours at Cowlairs as the rope on the incline broke before all the carriages could be hauled up. It was rumoured that those hostile to the line had cut it. However, haulage by a hemp rope on the Cowlairs incline would be a persistent problem.

The public services commenced on 21 February 1842 with four trains out and back between the cities; the 7am and 3pm called at all stations from Glasgow - Bishopbriggs, Kirkintilloch, Croy, Castlecary, Falkirk, Polmont, Linlithgow, Winchburgh, Ratho, Corstorphine and terminated at Haymarket. ('Kirkintilloch' is now Lenzie, while Castlecary, Winchburgh, Ratho and Corstorphine have gone). It would be August 1846 before the E&GR reached the centre of Edinburgh and constructed a station there.

Railways were the most complex organisations in the civilian domain that had ever existed and for their management military models were followed. Command structures were thus hierarchical. John Miller, the engineer for the E&GR, had advised that the railway should have departments to ensure its proper functioning. Therefore, a superintendent (later a general manager) should take charge of the whole establishment, a secretary of the offices, an engineer of the line, with another for the locomotives and workshops, and a goods clerk, subsequently a manager, should be responsible for the freight department. This advice was followed by the E&GR, with John Miller being retained for overall supervision of the railway for six months.

With timetables drawn up and approved by the directors, clocks had been ordered from Mitchell & Russell of Glasgow, one with a 'double face' for that terminus. For many people, these would be the first timepieces they would ever see and their proper regulation had to be considered – the time being taken from the Edinburgh Observatory, and sent by telegraph – making the correction for Glasgow some 4½

minutes after this, 'being within a few seconds of the exact difference'.

John Willox, who had accompanied Miller on a journey over the line just prior to its completion, now took an excursion to Glasgow. Approaching the town, he remarked on the huge chimney under construction at Tennant's St Rollox chemical works, a Glasgow landmark that would exceed 435ft (132.5m) in height. But another chimney also claimed attention – the one at the Engine House powering the incline cable, giving 'a fine effect upon the brow of the steep bank'. From there the train 'proceeds with great rapidity down the Tunnel through Bell's Hill, upwards of three-quarters of a mile in length, cut almost exclusively through rock, yet arched over, and brilliantly lighted with gas throughout its whole extent'.

There were further surprises as 'the astonished traveller finds himself transported into an almost faerie palace – this is the Passengers' Shed at the Glasgow terminus'. Willox goes on to extol the virtues of the structure – 'spacious and splendid ... elegant as well as commodious'. He also gives a useful description of the station 'furnished with a beautiful passengers' parade on each side' – that is platforms. The roof was supported on 48 cast iron columns arranged in double rows, the principal roof having a span of 64ft (20m). However, it was just a large timber shed, some 230ft (70m) in length and 85ft (25m) wide overall. There was also a 'splendid Booking Office, with access to waiting rooms with every

other convenience for the accommodation of travellers'. He did not mention any goods facilities – 'luggage trains' had yet to commence. By 1844 'several extensive, well aired GRANARIES and WAREHOUSES, at the Glasgow Station of the Edinburgh & Glasgow Railway' were advertised 'to let'. These facilities would become a source of persistent complaint by the town council.

The passenger business on the E&GR was soon much in excess of estimates, reaching almost double the daily volume predicted. Compared with the stagecoaches, first class rail travel to Edinburgh at 9 shillings was less than the cost of an inside seat on a coach, second class at 6s 6d less than that of an outside seat, and third class just 4s. While coaches took 5 hours between the cities, railways had a competitive edge with their speed of 2¼ hours by 'swift train'. When they began moderating their fares, passenger traffic increased rapidly. By the early 1840s, there were half fares for under 12s making family travel attractive. But the poor had little encouragement to travel by rail until the Railway Regulation Act of 1844 obliged companies to run Parliamentary trains at one penny a mile – often at inconvenient times and in vehicles without roofs – but the 'labouring classes' at last also got some benefit from railways.

Chapter 2

Serving a Growing City

With the opening of the Edinburgh & Glasgow Railway the citizens of the ambitious and rapidly growing city of Glasgow were able to exercise their new enthusiasm for rail travel. The consequence was that Queen Street station would soon become busier than had ever been anticipated.

Although there was a booking office with access to waiting rooms and 'every other convenience' for the accommodation of travellers, the arrangements tried to take account of the rigid class distinctions of the time. There was resentment among some members of the upper classes that railways 'brought together such an objectionable mixture of people' – from which there was no escape on a station platform. Railways thus began to break down social barriers and would prove 'great levellers'. However, coping with the 'mixture' was addressed by railway companies offering different classes of carriage with a corresponding fare structure, and the E&GR followed the prevailing pattern – with first, second and third class being available initially. Station facilities reflected class distinctions with first and second class waiting rooms, with separate lavatory arrangements installed for male and female passengers.

Following the official opening at Queen Street, there were four trains out and back between the cities, with the 7am and 3pm calling at all stations. All trains had first and second class passengers, but the 7am and the 3pm also carried third class. The fare from Queen Street to Haymarket in third class was 4 shillings, and this 'bargain' was popular with Scots who were prepared to put up with the lack of comfort and protection in open vehicles. Fares were on a sliding scale – it was said that the mileposts by the lineside were designed to let passengers and staff know how far they had travelled and give reassurance about value for money. Horseboxes could be hired at 15 shillings per horse. For intermediate stations, fares were calculated *'nearly in proportion to the distance'* and passengers soon argued over the rates. It is not therefore surprising that the E&GR appointed a 'complainer' to respond to letters of criticism from dissatisfied travellers. Only the 11am and 5pm were 'quick trains' – 'expected to perform the journey in 2¼ hours, until further notice'.

Passenger traffic was soon exceeding expectations; in its first four months, the E&GR carried 205,268 passengers, well above the forecast of 340,00 a year that had appeared in the prospectus. By the summer of 1846, over 1 million were being conveyed annually giving receipts of £106,456 – but the greatest rise was in third class passenger numbers. Scots, including the well-to-do, were prepared to tolerate uncomfortable conditions if the tickets were cheap. In second class, the carriages had roofs, but the windows were unglazed causing cold and dusty blasts – 'wire gauze eye preservers' were advertised for passengers as a wise precaution. John Miller suggested fitting blinds for second class use, but these were seen as making the vehicles 'unsuitable for females'. Third class passengers expected to stand in open trucks in all weathers, though the elderly brought their own stools. Appeals were soon made for 'sitting boards' for thirds, and for glazed windows for second class carriages. First class was of course generously upholstered in similar fashion to the 'inside' on stagecoaches.

With the growth in passenger numbers, the arrangements for purchasing tickets and boarding a train at Queen Street soon left much to be desired. The booking office was reached

Edinburgh & Glasgow Railway second class carriages of 1842 had no windows – a cause of complaints. (Allan G Rodgers)

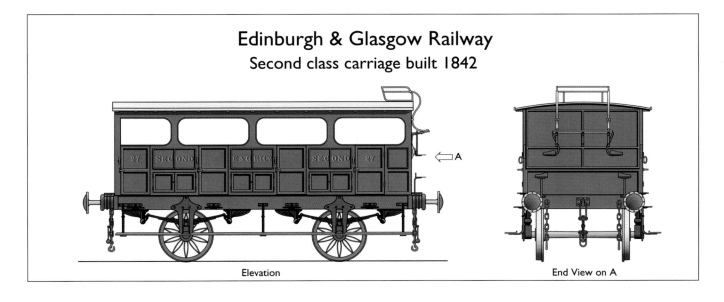

Edinburgh & Glasgow Railway
Second class carriage built 1842

Elevation End View on A

After the so-called Parliamentary trains began in 1844 with fares at 1d a mile, third class could be very congested as this sketch shows. By mixing social classes, the railway was a great leveller. (G F Allen collection)

With passenger numbers soaring in the 1840s, the inadequacy of arrangements for purchasing tickets was soon apparent at Queen Street and at many other stations. (Mr Punch's Railway Book – Project Gutenberg)

through a narrow dark passage where one clerk was assigned exclusively to first class leaving a solitary clerk to issue second, third and fourth class tickets (when that class became available after 1844):–

'Often when the man at the first-class table is standing looking on with his hands in his pockets, the place is in a state little better than the black hole of Calcutta. Amongst the crowd you may see respectable females, often with little children in their hands, hemmed in by huge Irish shearers, or other characters much less respectable. Of course, the strongest force their way through the tortuous passage, which has lately been constructed, apparently, for no other purpose than to increase the confusion, while the weak and helpless are obliged to submit to positive suffering till the way is cleared'. John Thomas in 'A Regional History of the Railways of Great Britain, Volume 6, Scotland'.

The conditions within the train shed were also unsatisfactory with the second and third class carriages standing in the tunnel where

passengers had to negotiate the narrow space between the tunnel wall, now blackened with soot, and the vehicles to find their seats. In spite of such conditions, special trains proved popular – for instance, the Highland & Agricultural Society members travelled to a dinner in Glasgow and the Mechanics' Institute in Glasgow went to Edinburgh. Parties of students were conveyed 'outwards at full fare and back free' as were supporters of temperance societies – a major social issue.

A vexed issue was the running of Sunday trains and this became inextricably linked with the carriage of the Royal Mail. In 1838, 'The Railways (Conveyance of Mails Act) stated that the mail should be carried by ordinary or special trains 'as required by the Postmaster General'. By 1841 the E&G directors feared that this might compel them to run Sunday trains, but they faced a dilemma as Sabbatarian views were entrenched in Scotland. Nevertheless, the carriage of Royal Mail was profitable for railways, and charges were negotiable. So the E&G directors offered to carry mail between the cities for £700 a year, an inflated sum that proved unacceptable, the Post Office arguing that the same amount should be paid as for the horse-drawn mail coaches – just £198 per annum.

In March 1842, the Postmaster General asked the E&G directors when a Royal Mail service could commence, and at what times of the day or night. Queen Street station would be a receiving point. The E&GR then became embroiled *'in a confused warfare of theology, economics, social concerns and politics',* according to historian C J A Robertson. The General Assembly of the Church of Scotland made its ministers' protests known when a deputation met the E&GR directors. Church interests were outraged and organised campaigns took place, with congregations, kirk sessions, presbyteries and synods joining the fray. Support for their position came from many town councils and lay organisations. Petitions attracted thousands of signatures. A flood of pamphlets argued 'for' and 'against' Sunday trains. Their running or abandonment was also regularly debated at the E&GR shareholders' meetings. Should trains be permitted as acts of mercy or necessity? Such was the agitation that John Leadbetter, the E&G chairman and its guiding light, who opposed Sunday trains, resigned in August 1842.

The E&GR's English shareholders were disconcerted as many favoured Sunday trains, and some Scots were also in favour – among these were the Town Councils of Bathgate, Greenock, Leith, Linlithgow and Paisley. Sundays were the only days when people did not go to work, and therefore gave the possibility of visiting family or having an excursion. Opportunities also came on Fast Days, the

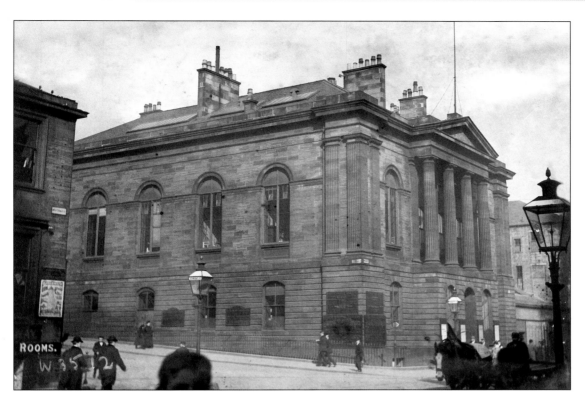

The Congregational Chapel, in classical style on West George Street, subsequently became the Head Office for the E&GR. (Glasgow Museums & Libraries Collections)

holidays prior to twice-yearly Communions, when people were freed from their daily labours.

Nevertheless, the E&GR had to conform to the Act obliging the railway to convey mail – so there had to be a compromise. Consequently, there would be only two trains on a Sunday, at 8am and 5pm carrying mail. These times did not interfere with divine services, thereby allowing both travellers and 'company servants' to attend church. On weekdays, Royal Mail would be conveyed on the 11am trains with stops only at Castlecary, Falkirk and Linlithgow. However, the protests against Sunday trains persisted leading to their complete cessation 'on or after Sunday 15 November, 1846', the only exceptions being emergencies. There would be no resumption of such trains until the E&GR was absorbed by the North British Railway in July 1865.

By the mid-1840s railway company reports were revealing just how convenient and profitable lines could be. Railways were expanding economic activity and were becoming major industries in their own right. Through their speed of communication, lines were having a phenomenal effect – as the rails advanced, distances for travelling simply shrank. However, a 'free for all' of railway development had to be restrained and in 1844 Parliament passed a Railway Act when William Gladstone, a politician with Scottish ancestry, was President of the Board of Trade. This not only attached conditions to the construction of railways but, under new laws, carriages had to be 'covered', preferably with roofs to give some protection, and passengers must have seats. To restrain overcharging, railway companies had to provide

The Parcels Office for the E&GR was accessed by a lane from West George Street The timber shed of the first station is visible. (Glasgow Stations, J R Hume & C Johnston)

on each of their lines 'conveyance for Third Class passengers' at the cost of one penny a mile, at least once a day in each direction – the so-called 'Parliamentary trains'. Their average speed was to be not less than 12 miles per hour (19km/h). The Act also warned railway companies about a state takeover of railways if they did not cooperate.

In 1844 'Railway Mania', a massive speculation in railway company stock and the promotion of new lines, had begun to sweep Britain, The attraction of joint-stock companies with the prospect of high interest rates lured people with money to spend (and many less wealthy) into a speculative frenzy. With profits coming from factories, the new middle class had funds available for investment. Government bonds, long thought 'safe' were now much less rewarding than railway stock – this was yielding 5 per cent or more – a prospect that made investors, typically in Lancashire, enthusiasts for railway shares and the 'Railway Mania' began.

By 1845 Bills had been drawn up for 110 Scottish schemes alone, each having a

Engineering ingenuity where the tunnel from the Caledonian Railway's Buchanan Street station cut under the Port Dundas branch (Forth & Clyde Canal) and topped the Cowlairs tunnel of the E&GR – shown by the relieving arch in the retaining wall at Buchanan Street station.

of the British rail network had largely been defined – though only about half of the tracks had actually been laid.

The months of intense speculation led railway companies to make deals that had long term effects, some of which would produce junctions with friendly lines. If hostility was encountered, then extracting running powers might be an option, or a company might lay claim to territory for a line of its own, thereby blocking the opposition. Greenhill, in mid-Scotland, soon became a strategic place on the developing network. By March 1848 the Scottish Central Railway had formed a junction with the E&GR there; this resulted in through running for the SCR to and from Queen Street station with more trains than ever using its limited facilities. Soon the Caledonian Railway, coming north from Carlisle, would cross under the E&GR and meet the SCR, and its trains also made use of Queen Street for many years.

With train numbers on the increase, the Cowlairs Incline was soon proving a headache with rope haulage causing recurring problems. The heavy hemp rope was installed on a system of pulleys on the up line out of Queen Street station. Made in Newcastle, it was 4,840 yd (4425m) in length, reported to be 6in (15cm) in circumference and weighed 24 tons. A contemporary description stated that 'the trains are drawn up the incline by an endless rope... carried upon guide pulleys ...at a rate usually of 12 miles per hour which is slow motion if the train is light ...but this rate may, however, be increased to 20 miles an hour'.

The action of the endless rope was dependent on the two beam engines in the engine house at Cowlairs. These had 28in (71cm) cylinders and 72in (182 cm) stroke. The crankshaft had a 12ft (3.6m) diameter spur wheel that drove an 18ft (5.4m) main cable drum through gearing; this drum was mounted in a pit excavated below the track level. The beam engines were powered by no fewer than 8 boilers, supplying steam at 50psi.

To access the haulage system at Queen Street, trains waited at the tunnel mouth, where a chain and messenger rope was hooked on to the locomotive's front buffer beam. Two brake wagons were attached with a slip coupling at the rear of the train. Communication with the engine house at Cowlairs was maintained by the electric telegraph. From its opening, the E&GR took pride in being an 'electric' railway – the electric telegraph on posts and wires was installed along its linesides. When a bell rang in the engine house, a horn was blown at Cowlairs to confirm that the message had been received, and the ponderous beam engine was set in motion. The haulage of the locomotive and train up through the tunnel could then begin. Meanwhile, on the

prospectus setting out the potential gains in glowing terms. Hopeful investors pored over newspapers and such journals as the *Scottish Railway Gazette* while stocks and shares in railway companies were traded at ridiculous prices. By 1846, 'The Railway Shareholder's Manual or Practical Guide to the Railways of the World' had reached its 7th edition. When the speculative bubble burst that year, there were heavy financial losses for some investors as there was no limited liability at that time – whereupon enthusiasm for railway projects declined and construction was often postponed.

Much money went on expenses – there were outlays for promoting lines and devising a prospectus, on paying engineers for carrying out surveys and drawing up plans, and in covering lawyers' fees for taking Bills to Parliament – and not on any lines at all. In 1845, Parliament passed Acts for 2,816 miles of railway, potentially absorbing capital of £40 million, before the 'bubble burst'. Yet by 1 January 1849, the shape

The double-beam engine for the Cowlairs Incline with George Jack, the engineer who operated the system for many years. (The Engineer, 1922)

The method of attachment of the incline cable to the front buffer beam of a locomotive. (NBRSG Archive)

footplate the enginemen would aim to create a good head of steam – in order to outpace the haulage rope at the top of the incline. Here the messenger rope would drop off the front buffer beam as the locomotive ran ahead with its train. Getting up speed in the tunnel caused both smoke and steam in abundance that the two 'eyes', or ventilation shafts did little to reduce. It was an endurance test for the enginemen, but

also for the second and third class passengers in vehicles without any glazing.

To descend the incline, trains stopped short at Cowlairs where the locomotive was detached. The brakemen in their 14ton brake wagons now took charge. Then the train engine would run round the carriages nudging them into motion on the brow of the hill. It was the job of the brakemen to take the train down the incline by gravity but under control with wooden brake blocks, and bring it to a halt on the short stretch of level track in Queen Street station.

In July 1844 the first of several incidents involving the Cowlairs incline was reported to the Board of Trade. A train of eleven wagons was carrying building stone from quarries at Bishopbriggs to Glasgow, and the speed of its descent could not be arrested. Once out of the tunnel, the train crashed into the station house, continued through the parcels office, broke

This plan for an extension at Queen Street station and proposed open cuttings of the tunnel is dated 1855. (Glasgow City Archives, Mitchell Library)

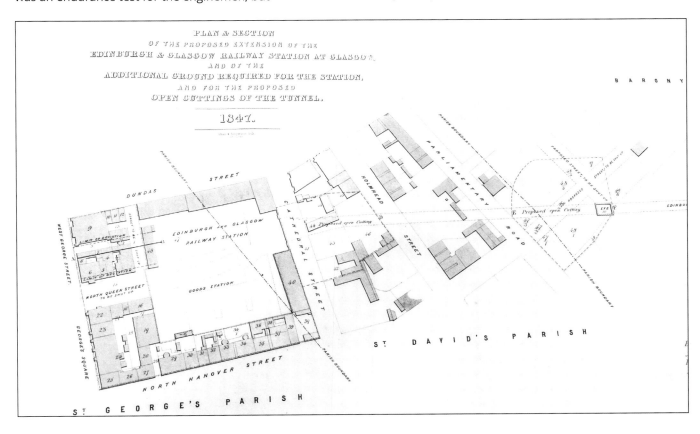

PLAN & SECTION
OF THE PROPOSED EXTENSION OF THE
EDINBURGH & GLASGOW RAILWAY STATION AT GLASGOW,
AND OF THE
ADDITIONAL GROUND REQUIRED FOR THE STATION,
AND FOR THE PROPOSED
OPEN CUTTINGS OF THE TUNNEL.

1847.

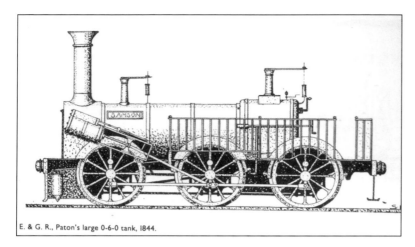

E. & G. R., Paton's large 0-6-0 tank, 1844.

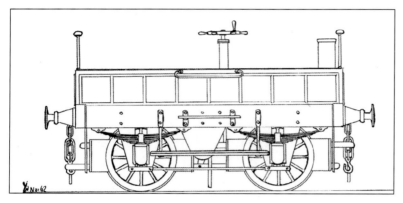

Problems with rope haulage on the Cowlairs Incline led to banking engines being tried between 1844 and 1847. This locomotive is 'Samson', built at Cowlairs.
(S.Everard in NBRSG Journal)

The Cowlairs brake wagons were robustly constructed with floors of cast iron slabs and brake blocks on each wheel. Brakemen controlled hand brakes on central pillars. (John Thomas, The North British Railway, Vol.1)

through the facing wall and 'traversing the carriageway in front of the station, came against the building opposite, the wall of which was a little injured'. This was in West George Street where the trucks and 'break' piled up and were 'much broken'. Remarkably, as long as the inclined plane was in use, there were no serious accidents to passengers at Queen Street station.

After less than six months usage, by July 1842, a heavier rope was seen as the answer to breakages. Then in March 1843, a radical proposal was made – locomotives would be used to bank trains up the tunnel from Queen Street. An energetic and innovative locomotive superintendent William Paton had been appointed to take charge of the Cowlairs workshops. Two heavy tank engines were therefore designed and constructed there, appropriately named *Hercules* No.21 and *Samson* No.22

These tank engines had ingenious devices - hot water could be sprayed on the rails in the tunnel to loosen oil and grease, and cold water jets then washed the debris off. At the time, they were reckoned the most powerful locomotives ever built. Introduced in January 1844, a visitor had a trip up the incline on the 'driver's platform' aboard one of the 'puffing monsters' in February. It was a race at 20mph with a train of 17 little carriages. With Paton driving, it took only 5 minutes to reach Cowlairs, while the descent was 'perfectly under the control of the brakes'. Nevertheless, the engines soon caused

problems; their weight of 22 tons fractured the light tunnel rails while the blast of their powerful exhausts was alleged to damage the tunnel roof – seepage had to be deflected by lead sheeting taking the water to the trackside gutters.

Altogether, the banking experiment was disappointing, being abandoned in March 1847 when the enginemen, rope splicers and brakemen were called back to work. As for the tank engines, one was adapted for goods haulage, showing its strength on trains of 60 to 100 laden wagons at night without assistance.

At Glasgow, 'the want and inconvenience' at Queen Street station were already the subject of complaints, but the other terminals were also deficient. By 1846 four Parliamentary Select Committees were followed by a Royal Commission to consider a range of schemes for new termini for both passengers and goods traffic in the city. 'The Glasgow Central Terminus Commission' was chaired by Captain Coddington of the Board of Trade, and it investigated the possibility of a central station where all the city's lines should converge.

The E&GR, with its 1million passengers annually, estimated that 60 to 80 per cent went through Queen Street station. It now handled much E&G goods traffic, of which 30,000 tons went to the Broomielaw for onward shipping. An E&GR employee was asked the obvious, "Is your present station too small for your traffic?" He answered, "it is almost unworkable from the smallness of the accommodation and the great increase in traffic".

John Leadbetter, the company's former chairman, explained the inconvenience for passengers of having to cross busy city streets to get from Queen Street to Bridge Street for the Ayr and Greenock lines, or to the Broomielaw for the steamers. Timetables were not integrated between the E&GR and the south bank lines, and so there were "numerous instances of parties, with servants and children, and others who had to look after their luggage, arriving just in time to be too late". There was frequent disappointment when trains were delayed, or steamers were missed. To cross the city, a cab cost one shilling, with 2d for tolls, a porter to carry luggage was one shilling; a solitary omnibus was popular as there was no charge for luggage.

Despite the arguments, the Commissioners' Report in 1847 supported the status quo. Information about local and through traffic had been sparse, and improving links between the existing stations was seen as very difficult. Adequate terminal stations for *local traffic* should be the prime concern as for most people the city was their destination. Queen Street station's advantage was its location, 'a convenient spot for passenger traffic to the north and east', though it was admittedly 'too small'.

The E&G directors realised that improvements there had to be faced. In February 1847 a letter had come from a proprietor in George Square about a site between Queen Street and Hanover Street available for £18,750 – a price at first rejected as 'too high'. Nevertheless, the seller persisted and in early March disclosed that 'the offer would not be binding on him after 4 o'clock that day'. The purchase was made backed by a loan from Scottish Union Insurance, and funds from a bond on a George Square property. The following April, a station extension at North Queen Street was being considered.

By this purchase, the E&GR found itself the owner of the Wellington Hotel and the company retained Mrs Cotton, the tenant there. The business was worrying – if the roof leaked or the stove was deficient, a reduction in rent was requested, but the Cotton tenancy lasted until the 1850s. When the E&GR opened, there were only four hotels or inns in the vicinity of George Square, but by 1848 there were seven, a result of its presence. One of these had the prescient name, 'North British Hotel'.

With the Cowlairs Incline proving a persistent problem, by 1847 yet another solution was being tested – wire rope. Its inventor was Robert

Stirling Newall who was born in Dundee in 1812. He developed a machine for making wire ropes with several strands and by 1840 had taken out a patent. A factory was opened at Gateshead and in February 1847, a 4½ in (11.4cm) wire rope, weighing 15 tons and costing £840 was installed on the incline. Some alterations – not to exceed £2,500 – were also made to the beam engine. William Paton urged its simplification – two operating speeds of 12 and 20 mph were proving complex, but the lower speed was permanently used and this could not cope with

Between Queen Street and Bridge Street stations, cabs and omnibuses transported passengers, as seen in this view of the Trongate. (Scottish Cities)

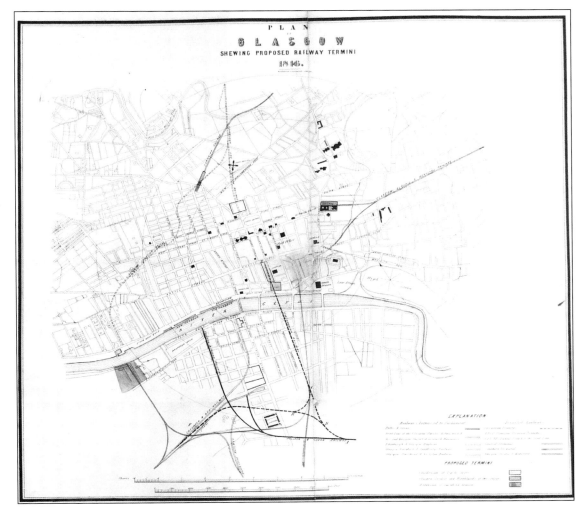

A plan showing a proposed arrangement of railways and termini in the City of Glasgow in 1846. (National Records of Scotland)

A wire rope was used on the Cowlairs Incline from 1847; here the rope is being replaced c1900 with a new supply on a wagon. (North British Railway Album)

12 loaded carriages, small though these were. With revised gearing, he hoped for 15mph. A steam brake would be fitted to a spare wheel on the crankshaft – a device to act instantly 'as the screw (*brake*) never answered', a disquieting admission.

Paton also suggested alternating the wooden pulleys in the tunnel with more robust iron ones at 80ft (24m) intervals. Such modifications did not overcome the difficulty of getting trains out of Queen Street station, where as the engineer said, 'a deal of time is lost in pushing the Train up to attach the Rope' – as this could not be taken beyond the 'offsets', those lines accessing the sidings to the station's goods yard on its east side. Meanwhile, John Miller had suggested opening out much of the tunnel – but the cumbersome haulage on the incline would continue for another sixty years.

There was another accident on the incline in September 1847 when the 11pm goods train from Edinburgh with twenty loaded trucks was approaching Queen Street. Thirteen empties were also requested there. The train went down the incline in two parts but 'between the bridges, the loaded portion overtook the empty trucks' and the brakemen and guard were knocked down by the impact. The brakes were ineffective, the train racing down the tunnel out of control, struck a wall and entered a store at the station. The guard and one brakeman jumped clear but the other was fatally injured.

Though only two Mail trains were run on Sundays, a flow of objections continued with the directors receiving many protests. The Surveyor of the GPO instructed that the night mail trains should depart both Edinburgh and Glasgow at 10pm and arrive not later than 12.45 at

Edinburgh – extra time being allowed for climbing the incline from Queen Street. These trains could also carry goods, plus first and second class passengers. Traffic that would become significant was the newspaper trade and such parcels could now be put on trains 'up to the hour of starting of the last Train at night'.

The desire of Glasgow and Edinburgh people to explore each other's cities brought surges of traffic, notably at the Glasgow Fair in July. Over three days, extra morning and evening trains were arranged for this traditional holiday. 'Cheap pleasure trips' were reported to do 'a great stroke of business' for the railways. Though there were temperance issues, 'not more than two per cent of the people were affected with liquer (sic)'. Special events, such as gatherings of the Grand Lodge of Scotland, had attention with single fares for return journeys – if they could guarantee 200 passengers.

Soon the term 'Express Train' appeared and Anglo-Scottish services became possible using the North British and associated East Coast companies. Queen Street station became a starting point. From June 1847, passengers joining the 5.20am train there were at Edinburgh by 6.43am, Berwick by 8.15am, Newcastle by 11.30am and York by 2.20pm, arriving in London at 9pm. The 5.20am also allowed passengers to reach Manchester at 6pm and Liverpool at 8pm the same day. A service leaving at 2.15pm was linked to a train reaching London at 8am the following morning. There was also a regular first class only service at 10am from Queen Street to York. Such opportunities transformed travel for Scots. Soon hand-written paper tickets were given up by the E&GR and a licence for the Edmondson system of card tickets was purchased. Such tickets would continue in use on BR until 1990.

Long distance travel led to the abandonment of local time arrangements. By 1847 the leading English railway companies had announced that they would use Greenwich Mean Time, a move supported by the Corporations of Liverpool and Manchester. The E&GR then urged the Lord Provosts of Glasgow and Edinburgh to follow and the acceptance of GMT made nationwide timetables possible.

With E&G stations, particularly Queen Street, being viewed by travellers as 'uncomfortable and chaotic', by 1848 an alternative way to travel was available – by the Caledonian Railway. Revenue fell when a price war began with the CR offering cut-price tickets from Glasgow to Edinburgh via Carstairs – even though its best train over this lengthy route – compared with 42 miles on the E&G – took much longer. There was also unrest among E&G staff when wages were cut and booking clerks at Queen Street resigned.

A positive investment, for the safety of the

railway and its passengers was the telegraph. By 1850, the early installation had been replaced by the Electric Telegraph Company's equipment, and in addition to train movements, personal messages could be sent from stations at a cost of half a guinea (10s 6d). It took only 5 minutes to transmit a message from Queen Street to another station, and soon these could be relayed to London over 520 miles away by the joint efforts of seven railway companies and news could be sent across the nation within hours.

Smoking was strictly forbidden 'both in and upon the Carriages and in the Company's Stations', where the penalty was 'not exceeding Forty Shillings'. Good behaviour was expected of passengers, 'the Commission of any other Nuisance in Carriages, Stations or Premises' met with a penalty of £5; failure to pay for a ticket risked a fine or imprisonment and for intoxication and riotous conduct', the penalty was similar.

The E&GR had problems that echo modern difficulties, such as the challenge of 'working traffic with only half the engines the company possessed'. An innovation was tried in October 1848 when 'Crampton's Improved Locomotive Engine' was tested on the E&GR. Thomas Russell Crampton designed a type of engine with a low boiler and large driving wheels. A simple driving axle was placed below the firebox giving the engines a low centre of gravity and they were considered safe at high speeds, some said to log 75mph. The engine left Queen Street 'at eight o'clock on an experimental trip to Edinburgh':–

'The morning was drizzling and the rails were in so greasy a state that it had by no means a fair trial. Mr Crampton, and four gentlemen went on the tender, so that the particular excellencies of the new patent locomotive might be better seen'.

– Glasgow Herald 9 October 1848

Good time was maintained, the run being 'highly satisfactory'. However, Cramptons did not appear on the E&G, proving less popular in Britain than on the continent. The E&G's motive power was clearly inadequate as on its near level route, 9 per cent of the trains were 'assisted' by pilot engines. Even so, in March 1847, when 520 trains were run, only 30 failed to keep time, 12 were 'late but not over 5 minutes' and only 2 were 'beyond 15 minutes'.

The costs of running a railway were worrying. To increase E&G revenue, it was suggested that vacant ground above the tunnel at Glasgow should be enclosed and let for development. The E&GR's rolling stock was also deficient, the third class and 'stand ups' being 'in a very bad state from frequent exposure to rain'. The water for locomotives at Cowlairs – serving both as works and as a depot for Queen Street station traffic – was 'both bad and scarce'. After an

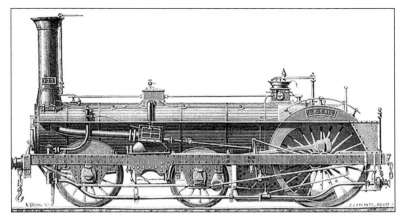

A Crampton designed 2-2-2 locomotive was tested on the E&GR in 1848 but the style was not adopted by the company. (Old book illustrations)

accident to a private hire near Ratho, a judge stated that to improve safety, the condition of engines and their mode of working should be examined before their use. Rules for the qualifications and appointments of 'Enginemen, Guards, Policemen and others on all Railways' had already come within the Railway Regulation Act of 1844. 'Policemen' in this context were signalmen – which explains why they became known as 'bobbies'.

Unless railway companies made agreements with a local constabulary, they soon had to recruit men to check criminality in and around stations. Stations were 'places of popular resort' where luggage could prove tempting. Gentlemen were prone to have gold watches stolen. Pick pocketing was troublesome – the Marchioness of Bute losing a gold thread purse and money at Queen Street in March 1849.

On 17 August 1849 a royal visit to Glasgow– the first by a reigning monarch for over 200 years – took place. The royal party may have had some trepidation as 1848 was a year when republican revolts against European monarchies affected France, Germany and the Austrian Empire. In Britain, there had been on-going Chartist agitation, the key aim being 'universal manhood suffrage', or simply 'votes for men'; this had caused riots in Glasgow. Nevertheless, the royal visit became a cause for civic celebration on a grand scale and recognition of the growing importance of the city as a trading hub and industrial centre.

When Queen Victoria, accompanied by Prince Albert and their four children, disembarked from the steam yacht 'Fairy' at the Broomielaw's south side, the Bridge Street Station of the 'Ayrshire Railways' came into view. No publicity tricks were missed here as the building was 'splendidly and tastefully' decorated with flowers and evergreens while a small engine was active in the station – features that the royal party commented upon.

After crossing the bridge at the Clyde, where sailing ships were dressed over all with their crews on the yardarms, the carriage procession reached Jamaica Street. Here an elaborate stone

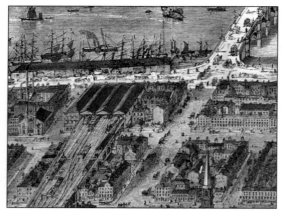

An aerial sketch from 1864 of Bridge Street station, showing its offices, sheds and track layout, and the quayside at the Broomielaw. (T. Sulman/Special Collections, Glasgow University Library).

arch surmounted by a crown, designed by the architect J H Rochead, had been erected. In Buchanan Street, there were balconies and stands so packed with spectators that the Queen rose up in her carriage and waved her handkerchief to the crowds. A band, attempting to play the national anthem, was drowned out by the cheering. In George Street, a large platform at Dr Wardlaw's Chapel, adjacent to Queen Street station, was filled with the 'fashionably dressed', and flags, flowers and draperies with the initials 'VR' adorned buildings in George Square. Pupils from the Ragged School and from the Deaf and Dumb Institute, evidence of the citizens' social conscience, looked on. The University, at the old College in the High Street, and the Cathedral were visited before the royal party returned via Trongate and Argyll Street to Queen Street station, 'amid crowds of people of every rank'.

Arrangements at the Edinburgh & Glasgow terminus for the royal party's departure were 'admirable' – 'a very elegant triumphal arch, occupying the whole width of the street, had been painted to resemble stone and a tall obelisk on top carried the royal standard' while arches of evergreens stood at the Dundas Street entrance. The wooden shed for passengers had been repainted and red cloth spread on the floor. On the platform, seats were set out for

'friends of the directors ... a galaxy of beauty and fashion ... admitted by ticket'. Beside the First Class Ticket Office, a retiring room had been fitted up 'with great taste' for the royal party. (An observer noted that it was just the First Class Ladies Waiting Room given an overhaul). Fruit, wine and cake were on offer; a 'handsome mirror' and 'the usual toilet conveniences' were also available. An adjoining room had refreshments for the royal suite. Ten directors were on hand, plus John Latham, the general manager, other staff and the engineer William Paton.

The royal train consisted of three first class carriages, plus a second class vehicle with a van next the engine. In the middle first class carriage, a compartment had been fitted up with 'fawn striped silk cushions with arm rests in blue satin'. With bouquets presented, the Queen and her family quickly boarded. The directors saw them off and the platform party cheered until the train disappeared into the tunnel. The locomotive was '*Orion*', a Cowlairs built 2-2-2, and on the footplate, its designer, William Paton took charge. All along the E&GR, men had been placed at short intervals to ensure that the line was clear. In fact, the reporter 'had never seen any similar occasion in which all the details were so complete and perfectly satisfactory'.

With the Cowlairs Incline safely surmounted, the train was soon at Greenhill Junction – according to the report in 20 minutes. This was where the E&GR system met the Scottish Central Railway. There the chairman and directors of the latter company were waiting and after a brief delay, with a fresh engine 'affixed to the train', it set off on the SCR for Perth. The royal family spent the night in the George Hotel. The following day, the journey north was completed by coach. Although half the distance might have been covered by rail, the Queen preferred 'posting' from Perth as it allowed her to see and be seen. A weary Queen made no comments in her 'Journal' about the railway, only mentioning that she was told that 400,000 people had viewed her in Glasgow. Subsequently, a handsome equestrian statue of the monarch was placed in George Square, and the George Hotel was re-named the Queen's Hotel.

By 1851 'Rules and Regulations' were drawn up and issued to E&GR employees who had to vouch for having read them, or had them read to them, before signing the booklet. These must be carried at all times or a penalty of five shillings paid. Instructions should be obeyed promptly – incivility, rudeness or use of improper language was not tolerated. Intoxication brought dismissal. Employees should be neat and clean, reporting anything that might affect 'the safe and proper working of traffic'. Everyone must know the terms 'Up' to Edinburgh and 'Down' to

On the royal visit to Glasgow in 1849, Queen Victoria, Prince Albert and their children disembarked from a steam yacht at the Broomielaw. (Illustrated London News)

Glasgow. Strict attention must be given to 'Danger and Caution Signals' – responsibility for these resting with those exhibiting them. All orders and instructions should be written if possible, and any order received verbally must be repeated – to ensure that it was properly understood.

Tourism was growing and railways were increasingly seen as a 'safe' means of travel. Thomas Cook was a pioneer of travel for pleasure, first running an excursion in the Midlands in 1841 and soon having an office in Edinburgh. As early as 1848, 'travellers for pleasure' were reported to be benefiting E&GR business. By 1850 several editions of Black's 'Economical Tourist of Scotland' had been published. The E&GR was soon offering tours of the Highlands in the summer months; these excursions were planned to meet different income and interest levels. The starting point for several was Queen Street station. One tour had tickets available for four days and featured the Trossachs, Loch Katrine and Loch Lomond. Travel by rail, steamer (cabin class) and outside on a coach cost 17s 6d. From 1858, Callander, a gateway to the Trossachs, could also be reached by train, and a tour of the Southern Highlands cost 30s for a week. Travellers could now explore 'Rob Roy' country made famous in the writings of Sir Walter Scott; the great novelist is attributed with starting tourism in Scotland based on its heritage and environment.

There was an expansion of branches served from Queen Street – the E&G's Campsie branch was set for extension along the Blane Valley at a cost of £35,000, a line for which the E&GR was willing to subscribe £15,000; Campsie Glen, with its waterfalls and inn, was a popular venue. For access to the Clyde coast and lochs, the Glasgow, Dunbarton & Helensburgh Junction Railway was advancing with plans for a pier at Helensburgh, but an eye had to be kept on the rival Caledonian & Dumbartonshire Junction Railway that was also aiming for the coast and Loch Lomond shores. From 1851 a daily newspaper, 'The North British Daily Mail' was on sale at Queen Street station and proved a useful means of advertising excursions.

Soon 'villa tickets' were introduced to encourage house building away from the towns but in places within a mile of any stations, such as Lenzie; the aim was to bring more passenger business to the railway through the year. First known as 'Kirkintilloch' by the E&GR, then as 'Campsie Junction', Lenzie was where the Campsie branch took off from the main line in what was then countryside. The number of villa tickets on offer was dependent on the value of a proposed property – a £500 house merited a free ticket for five years, but if the villa had already been built, the owner did not qualify.

Some relief from the congestion at Queen Street came in 1855 when the long desired West George Street Chapel – Dr Wardlaw's Kirk – became railway company property. This acquisition had called for persistence – another offer of £14,100 had been put on the table. As the congregation showed reluctance to quit, there would be an extra £600 to leave by Martinmas (November) 1855, but only £300 for vacating by Whitsun (June) 1856. There were other inducements as chapel members were given E&GR ticket concessions. When the chapel became the E&GR head office, 'being sent fur tae gang tae the kirk' could signal a reprimand or worse for railway employees. The 'kirk' stood as railway property for BR until the 1970s.

This purchase may have been the impetus for improving access to the station that was carried out at Dundas Street in 1855-6. There a five arch structure in sandstone with a heavy cornice and balustrade was erected. The slated roof was carried on a cast iron frame supported on a single column. Passenger access was now much better, and the station continued to be known as 'Dundas Street'.

By 1855 such was the growth of E&GR goods traffic that freight receipts were in excess of passenger receipts. Improving the goods station at Queen Street then became an issue and

A triumphal masonry arch to honour the Queen was erected at Jamaica Street, but the E&GR had to make do with a wooden structure and flags at Queen Street station. (Illustrated London News)

A first class E&GR carriage of this type took the royal party from Queen Street to Perth after the royal visit to Glasgow in 1849. (The Steam Museum, County Kildare, Ireland)

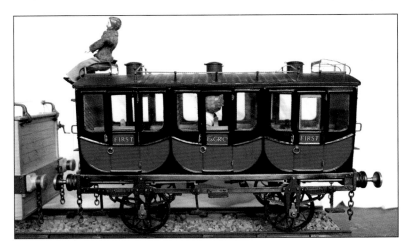

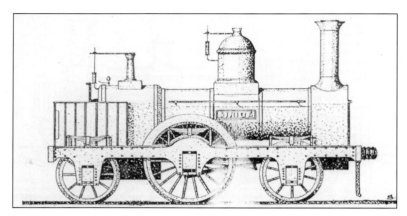

The locomotive used on the E&GR Royal Train was this 2-2-2 built at Cowlairs and named 'Orion'. (S.Everard, NBRSG Journal)

Cowlairs station with the prominent clock (left) and a B1 on an Edinburgh train in the LNER years. (Ian Allan Ltd)

thought was given to opening out and widening the tunnel up to Cathedral Street. This would have allowed the doubling of the goods sidings beside North Hanover Street – potentially increasing the volume handled to 1,000 tons a week or 50 extra wagons a day – but the existing facilities could not accommodate these all at once. The solution proposed was to take a line out of the tunnel to Parliamentary Road and to construct a new goods yard there. The estimated cost was £54,000 for land purchase and works, but the opportunity was not taken. Instead, the company chose to have more sidings at Cowlairs. By 1861, this location claimed to have the first purpose-built signal cabin in Scotland from which signals at a distance were worked by levers and wires. Cowlairs also now had a station. When new rails were laid in the Cowlairs tunnel, the task was done at night to minimise disruption to train services in and out of Queen Street station.

The E&GR began letting advertising space at stations – in addition to the posting of its own information about train services and fares. Displaying advertisements at its stations – at £100 a year – would be a useful revenue stream for the railway. The E&GR also used advertisements to 'name and shame' those who contravened its regulations, such as the sailor whose behaviour led to his appearance at the Sheriff Court in Linlithgow. However, placing advertisements in carriages was declined.

As railways were becoming more safety conscious, insurance for employees, especially guards, was under discussion. Ticket checking from the running boards along the sides of carriages was hazardous and guards had proposed that half of a premium should be paid by the E&GR. In 1858 The Railway Benevolent Institution was established to support railway staff, both active and retired, and to assist their dependents by preventing and relieving poverty. There was some reluctance about the E&GR's participation, but by 1860 employees' contributions were being logged on the pay sheet. An insurance company had a scheme for passengers in which the E&GR did take part – a policy could be purchased when a ticket was booked – the company paying one-third of the cost of a claim for injury or loss.

By the 1860s Queen Street station was badly in need of improvement. Its timber sheds and facilities were out of date and worn. Estimates showed that a new roof would cost £3,780 and the walls £400, but the expenditure was unacceptable. Some enhancement was tried – the interior of the roof was whitewashed and the urinals ventilated at a cost of just £95. To assist the arranging of trains, a traversing machine was investigated and Messrs Stevens, a company that would be synonymous with signalling, could supply points for £250.

In 1856 the purchase of 'splendid express engines' from Beyer Peacock of Manchester

transformed E&G motive power. Frequent complaints about 'detentions' of trains on the line had highlighted the weakness of old engines in keeping time. In 1864 William Stroudley, who would become a renowned locomotive engineer, was appointed manager of the E&GR works. He not only improved the construction and repair of locomotives and rolling stock, but also modified the incline's stationary engine and rope – finding that it 'only stood still for 12 hours on a Sunday'.

The E&GR's desire for railway expansion brought ever more business to Queen Street station. In 1860 tickets for overnight travel to an International Exhibition in London were advertised at £1, with first class by day at £4.

Above: Stone arches were built as the main station entrance in Dundas Street and adjoining the Wardlaw Chapel in 1855-6. This view dates from the 1950s. (J F McEwan)

Below left: The E&GR advertisements 'named and shamed' unruly passengers who could be fined or imprisoned. (National Railway Museum)

Below: Proposed enlargement of Queen Street station 'with ground to be acquired' in 1855. (National Records of Scotland)

EDINBURGH & GLASGOW
RAILWAY.
CAUTION.

JOHN WHITTON, Sailor, belonging to H.M. Ship "Jackall," Charged with being Drunk and Disorderly in the 2 p.m. Train from Edinburgh to Glasgow, on Saturday, the 4th July current, and with Annoying and Assaulting his fellow Passengers. He had to be taken from the Train at Falkirk Station, and was brought before Sheriff SCONCE, and Fined in the Sum of

5 Shillings,
Or Eight Days' Imprisonment.
BY ORDER.

COMPANY'S OFFICES,
GLASGOW, July, 1863.

M'CORQUODALE & CO., Printers, 83 Maxwell Street, Glasgow.

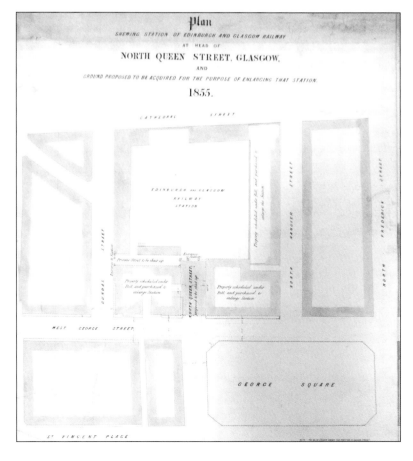

Plan
SHEWING STATION OF EDINBURGH AND GLASGOW RAILWAY
AT HEAD OF
NORTH QUEEN STREET, GLASGOW,
AND
GROUND PROPOSED TO BE ACQUIRED FOR THE PURPOSE OF ENLARGING THAT STATION.
1855.

The internal arrangements at Queen Street station in 1860 show alcoves for storing carriages on the west side with turnplates for access. (The North British Railway, Vol.1, John Thomas)

Inset far right: *The E&GR's Working Timetables for staff in 1864 prior to the company's absorption by the North British Railway. (National Records of Scotland)*

For the E&GR's, 0-4-2 locomotives from Beyer, Peacock of Manchester in 1859-62 were its last. No 90, after rebuilding, continued to 1912. (Euan Cameron)

Season tickets and 'pleasure party' rates were also on offer. Passenger comfort was not overlooked – there were left luggage facilities and bookstands at Queen Street. The E&GR now had responsibility for the Queen's Hotel in George Square; when 'hot water baths' were installed, the lessee asked for compensation for loss of custom during the work.

By 1864, Queen Street station was hosting trains to and from Helensburgh, Balloch and Dumbarton, from Lennoxtown and from Grangemouth, in addition to its Edinburgh services. The E&GR had hopes of amalgamating with the Caledonian Railway but it was not to be. On 5 July 1865, it did absorb the Monkland Railways that it had long desired, but by 1 August both became part of the North British Railway and a new chapter at Queen Street station began. This was a time of seismic shift in the organisation of the early Scottish railway system from which five distinct companies

emerged – the North British, the Caledonian, the Glasgow & South Western, the Highland and the Great North of Scotland Railways.

By taking over the E&GR, the North British Railway not only got access to Queen Street station in central Glasgow but also to Lanarkshire coalfields, to Clydeside industries, and to coastal waters on the western seaboard. It now had influence from its ownership of a large and strategic network in Scotland.

On the other hand, for the management of the E&GR and for Queen Street station, it was demotion – the head office would no longer be in Glasgow but in Edinburgh. The senior staff of the founding company faced uncertain employment, and in Glasgow business circles and among shareholders, there was consternation and disappointment about the loss of this pioneering railway enterprise.

Chapter 3

Improvements in the 1870s

Queen Street station, on its constricted site with just two platforms and the long and steep Cowlairs tunnel for access, had long been under strain, and in December 1865 a grand plan was unveiled by the North British Railway. A line was proposed from Sighthill to join the City of Glasgow Union Railway (now a joint venture between the NBR and the Glasgow & South Western Railway that had obtained its Act in July 1864). This line would continue to an impressive station with eight platforms lying E-W on the site at Queen Street. Lines running east along the north side of George Street would merge at High Street. The station frontage would have an imposing hotel facing George Square. Such a rail system could go west to link up with the 'hoped for' Stobcross to Maryhill line, thereby providing looped access for Dumbarton and Helensburgh trains. Possibilities for suburban services would be enhanced and the Cowlairs tunnel would be closed. The NBR board hoped to raise £1.6m through the issue of £10 preference shares for the project, but in this it was unsuccessful.

However, the NBR was not alone in plotting a new central station – the Caledonian Railway had the intention of constructing a terminus in central Glasgow – if it could obtain authority to cross the River Clyde. Similarly the Glasgow & South Western nurtured its own hopes for St Enoch. Shareholders' meetings took place – some investors had money in more than one company, but which one should they back? The policies of the rival companies' directors were questioned. The estimate for the NBR project, seen as 'aggressive', was £4.3m. Observers pointed out that the CR 'central station', for which it had long hoped, would be in close proximity to the NBR one – the latter's passengers 'crossing the road' to travel in their rival's trains, thus siphoning off revenue. The total cost to create three new termini in the city was put at over £10m, a sum calling for access to new capital that was simply not available. In March 1866, the 'grand plan' for Queen Street was abandoned with the concurrence of the Caledonian Railway.

The NBR had earlier constructed an expensive trunk line of its own to Carlisle – the Waverley Route that opened in July 1862. In that year the company had also expanded into Fife by taking over the Edinburgh, Perth & Dundee Railway. Such expansion endeavours under Richard Hodgson, an ambitious but unscrupulous chairman, strained the NBR's resources, leading to the third-rate and to spending cuts. The outcome was that locomotives, stations and track were in poor condition and requiring a great deal of money to be spent on them to achieve an efficient operation.

At NBR directors' meetings, discussion of accounts was often deferred. In fact, despite the regular, if small dividends, all was not well with the company's finances. By the autumn of 1866 the NBR was facing a funding crisis. Earlier in May of that year, the failure of the Overend Gurney bank in London had triggered a financial collapse when the economy went into recession and railway stocks were adversely affected. It soon emerged that the NBR's finances had been mismanaged for years and the practice of 'massaging' the accounts to gloss over deficiencies had become established. This was intended to give a positive impression to sustain shareholder confidence. To offer a modest return on investment and thereby support the NBR share price on the Stock Markets, interest on stock was being paid out of capital. When a new company secretary, 'blew the whistle', the scandal broke. The damage to the NBR's reputation was very serious, with Hodgson and

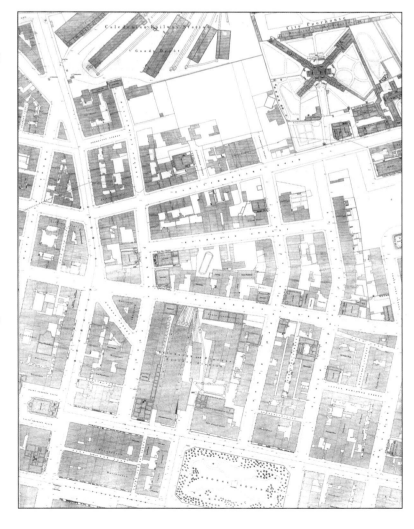

The Ordnance Survey Town Plan (1:500) of 1857 shows Queen Street station and its 'built up' surroundings prior to its reconstruction. (National Library of Scotland)

Above: *The Caledonian Railway's Buchanan Street station, a timber structure dating from 1850, took over running Caley trains to the north in 1870. (CR Association)*

Below: *An overview of the district north of George Square in 1864 shows Queen Street station with its timber sheds for passenger trains, goods yard and tall granary (lower right), and the Caley Buchanan Street station and goods yard (upper left). (T.Sulman/Special Collections/ Glasgow University Library)*

his fellow directors being forced to resign. A new board, committed to a policy of rigorous austerity, was chosen.

A Committee of Investigation discovered that 'misrepresentation, deception and the deliberate falsification of the accounts' had been the routine for years. Some shareholders were of the opinion that the directors should face imprisonment. This financial 'melt down' was to haunt the NBR for decades as investors did not readily forget its deceit. In 1867, the company's debt was £1.8m, a colossal amount at that date (about £60m at 2019 values).

From then on, the NBR faced economic rigour with spending on capital projects being viewed as 'pernicious'. The new directors felt compelled to accept only the lowest tenders and savings were urged wherever possible. When permanent way staff asked for topcoats and leggings, this was refused and the company's police were denied better uniforms. However, the tunnel pointsmen at Queen Street were given

overcoats. Scrap, whether old engines, surplus materials or rags, was sold for the best prices obtainable. The locomotive superintendent had to use his expertise to rebuild 'write off' engines. So miserly was the use of grease that there were frequent problems with the overheating of axle boxes – a deficiency of which the Board of Trade took note. Although hard bargains were driven for every item from coal supplies to rails, some small increases in wages and salaries had eventually to be allowed, probably to encourage men to stay with the NBR. The fact that the price of coal had risen was attributed to 'a great advance in miners' wages' with implications for NBR wage rates.

By the 1870s the North British Railway had a poor reputation for passenger comfort and convenience. Carriages were reported as dirty, trains as unpunctual and fares as too high. The NBR's flagship route of the E&G was a disappointing performer – the desire for fast running was spoiled by speed restrictions due to mining subsidence. Furthermore, the 'detentions' of passengers on its trains of 'comfortless shaking six wheelers' produced angry letters of complaint and hostile comments in the press.

How should the NBR react? How could the passenger experience be improved? In 1875 railway companies were challenged when the ambitious and wealthy Midland Railway offered superior comfort by placing third class passengers in second class carriages; this caused a sensation as these 'seconds' were 'upholstered' – an outcome that led to criticism that the MR 'pampered the working class'. (It would be 1892 before the NBR got rid of all its second class vehicles).

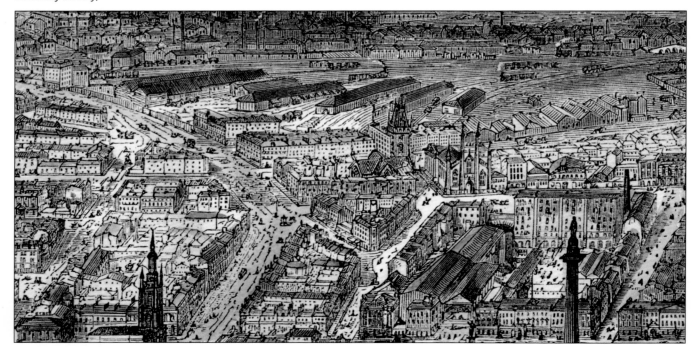

By 1 January 1870, the Caledonian Railway had completed extensions at its Buchanan Street station and CR trains bound for places north of Stirling ceased to use Queen Street station. This relieved pressures, but there was a downside – the NBR lost thousands of pounds that the CR had been paying for the privilege of using the premises, basic though these were.

The domestic arrangements at Queen Street station left much to be desired, but in 1871 these began to receive some attention – in the waiting rooms, the water closets would be 'cleaned out every morning and oftener if necessary', with 'chloride of lime', a powerful bleach produced by Tennants at their chemical works at St Rollox. A booking office screen 'up to roof level' at a cost of £5, and an extension to the lamp room at £45 were authorised. As the grain store was proving inadequate, £350 would be spent on extra accommodation as there was damage to grain 'exposed to the wet outside'.

The following year with business showing some improvement, 'advances and changes' were made to some staff salaries with £5 to £30 increases per annum. Some wages were also adjusted – the head office messenger got an increase of one shilling on twenty shillings a week, and porters, who largely relied on tips, also looked for better basic pay.

In its day, the E&GR had acquired premises that contained hotels. The Wellington was the first and its sitting tenant continued to run it, paying rent to the railway company. By 1871, it had been renamed the Queen's Hotel and the lease was scrutinised – there was an offer of £2,000 a year for 10 years from the current lessee 'with permission given for the NBR to use four rooms and a closet'. Another hotelier offered the same sum for 15 to 20 years', but the current lessee was preferred. Soon there was trouble with the drains – £50 was given in compensation, the work being done 'to the satisfaction of the company's engineer'. Eventually, in September 1875 the property was purchased outright by the NBR for £36,000 and shortly a new lease was agreed. Then the former tenant asked for compensation to cover improvements he had made to the premises. Running hotels was proving troublesome for the railway company.

The NBR saloon carriages that the company used on the East Coast services were disliked by its North Eastern and Great Northern Railway partners. With passengers enduring rough journeys, the NBR's solution was to fit longer springs on the vehicles, but overheating of axleboxes continued. On a lighter note, an invitation came from the directors of the Loch Lomond and Loch Long Steamboat Company for the NBR board to have a pleasure sail over the lochs – in what became an annual event for the directors.

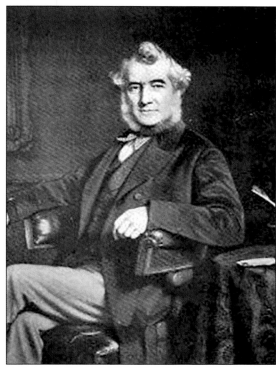

James Allport of the Midland Railway began a revolution in passenger comfort in 1876 by abolishing second class, thereby giving 'thirds' upholstered seats. (Project Gutenberg)

In November 1872, there were plans before the board for a proposed railway from Bothwell Street to the Helensburgh line (an echo of a Miller idea of the 1840s for taking a line under Blythswood Hill to the Clyde's north bank). The new proposal hinged on acquiring property for which parliamentary notice should be given. A conditional arrangement about sites was made whereby some £13,000 was paid to a Mr Scott to 'hold the position until Martinmas 1873'. A big question was whether Glasgow magistrates would ever permit a tunnel under the city and the stopping up of streets. Then came news of an unofficial plan being aired for the enlargement of Queen Street station and the improvement of Cowlairs tunnel, whereupon civil engineer T E Harrison, long associated with the North Eastern Railway and active in engineering consultancies, was called in 'to consider and advise on the proposed station accommodation at Glasgow'.

The inadequacies at Queen Street were only some of the adverse circumstances confronting the NBR directors. The Board of Trade had continuing reservations about the company's practices, especially its reluctance to have the block system with interlocking signals and points installed throughout the NBR. By 1874 only some 25 per cent of its network was so protected, but other railway companies were also dilatory. Railways were very dangerous places on which to be employed, a Royal Commission on Railway Accidents reporting that railway workers were a third more likely to suffer injury compared with other industrial workers in Britain.

In May 1876, with the Midland Railway having

*The first sleeping carriage in Britain was introduced by the North British Railway
at Glasgow Queen Street on through services to London Kings Cross in April 1873. (Engineering, 1873)*

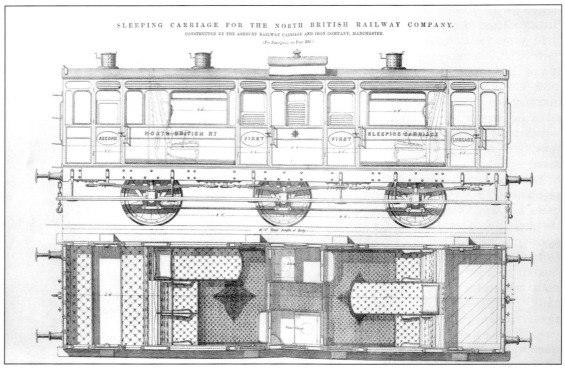

SLEEPING CARRIAGE FOR THE NORTH BRITISH RAILWAY COMPANY.
CONSTRUCTED BY THE ASHBURY RAILWAY CARRIAGE AND IRON COMPANY, MANCHESTER

completed its Settle& Carlisle route, through services began from London St Pancras to Edinburgh via the Waverley Route, and there were connections to Glasgow. The Midland's trains were slower than those of the East or West Coast companies, but it lured passengers by offering greater comfort with third class stock that was now *upholstered*. The NBR directors were discomfited over 'cushioning' in their vehicles and the extra costs that this entailed – and left the Stores Department at Cowlairs to try to sort matters out.

The Midland's innovative manager James Allport went further – to grow passenger business, first class fares would be cut to the former second class level. The company also introduced bogie coaches (with two sets of four wheels per carriage) that were much superior to the NBR's six-wheeled vehicles, both in interior appointments and in smooth running. Complaints about NBR time-keeping and about its comfortless 'shaking' rolling stock escalated. New orders for carriages were badly needed but the NBR had a debt of £28,000 (about £900,000 in 2019 values) with its supplier in Manchester that was awaiting settlement.

At Queen Street, the original long timber sheds, with smoke vents – aimed at clearing the air – still stood. Improving ventilation in the station would have been difficult in any case as Queen Street sat in a former quarry site. Even basic works – such as raising platform heights - were not attempted. The station itself continued to occupy a small footprint, and from the outset, the site had been too restrictive, with possibilities of serious expansion into adjacent areas well nigh impossible.

With adverse comments about Queen Street station, coupled with the poor standard of NBR services, what may be described as a 'charm offensive' to attract positive publicity was attempted. On 8 February 1873, 'The Glasgow Herald' reported the trial of *'The New Sleeping Carriage on the North British Railway'*. Regional newspapers from Dundee to London along the East Coast route, where the carriage would run, had been alerted and carried advance publicity for it. The six-wheeled vehicle had been constructed by the Ashbury Carriage and Iron Company Ltd in Manchester, and was a speculative purchase. It had two sleeping compartments, with their wooden interiors French polished and trimmed in crimson velvet with silver-plated fittings – though opulent, it was 'sombre grandeur'. There was also a washbasin and water closet– such facilities being exceptional on railway carriages at the time. A separate compartment for servants and storage for luggage completed the accommodation. Thick carpeting plus a patent underlay had been laid to quieten journeys, while India rubber had been used where the structure was fixed to the frames.

Prior to launching the sleeping carriage into service, the NBR directors summoned representatives from the rival Caledonian Railway to view the new vehicle in Queen Street station. There was a run over the E&G and a dinner for the participants to round off the day. While the invitees may have been impressed by the lavish interior, neither they nor the press were enthused by its potential. Nevertheless, when the NBR sleeping carriage set off from Queen Street station for London Kings Cross on

2 April 1873, it was the first 'sleeper service' in Britain. Passengers paid a 10s supplement (a hefty amount at that date) in addition to a first class ticket. Patronage was disappointing. With low passenger numbers, by January 1874 the NBR general manager was told to put the vehicle into East Coast Joint Stock for use between Glasgow, Edinburgh and London on alternate nights. Meanwhile, the Ashbury Company made repeated requests to have its account for £600 settled.

The West Coast partners were quick to respond to the challenge that the sleeping car presented, announcing in August 1873 that there was now a sleeping carriage on the Caledonian Railway, courtesy of the London & North Western, for overnight use on the West Coast route. However, the NBR sleeping carriage seemed to cause a stir in the south as in May 1878, Henry Oakley, the general manager of the Great Northern Railway, asked the NBR as an East Coast partner, to agree to three more sleeping carriages being added to the ECJS. The estimated cost was £600 to £700 each; without waiting for an answer, he ordered the vehicles by the end of the month. Sleeping cars transformed the misery of night journeys to or from Scotland, especially in winter for those who had to sit up:–

'the fatigue, the cold feet, the cramped muscles, the uneasy snatches of sleep and the futile attempts to read by the miserable light...' – Report in 'Staffordshire Sentinel'.

Some comfort was now available, but only for first class passengers – until the LNER introduced sleeping berths for third class in 1928.

As Queen Street station was such a dull hole, an attempt was made to improve its illumination with 'Bonner's Patent Gas Burners', but as these required 'a heavy pressure of gas', they were found 'unsuitable'. The fact that the station was poorly lit may have been a cause of the accidents that passengers suffered and for which compensation was claimed. At least, carriage cleaning was being tackled – by

Felix William Spiers (right) and Christopher Pond (left) were catering pioneers. From 1863 they began upgrading railway provision for passengers and had a contract with the NBR for the refreshment rooms at Queen Street. (Thomas Farrell)

combining this task with station duties and providing uniforms for staff.

In December 1874 a report came from the committee considering a new Queen Street station in Glasgow, but the directors' recommendation was again that no action be taken until the NBR was in a position to do such work on its own account. However, uncertainty about the station led to questions. The bookstall tenant was Thomas Murray, whose 'Murray's Diary' giving information about train services from Glasgow, would become well known. His offer of £300 a year topped John Menzies & Company's £280 – but he was warned that if the station was altered, the NBR could resume possession of the site without compensation.

Refreshment rooms were also likely to be affected by any station works. Both Queen Street and Waverley facilities were let to Spiers & Pond, the world's first major catering business that originated in the 1850s during the Australian gold rush. The partners set high

Dugald Drummond's new 2-2-2 locomotives built by Neilson at Springburn in 1876 soon featured on the E&G expresses with 70mph runs between the cities. (Euan Cameron)

© Euan Cameron

Dugald Drummond, the locomotive superintendent (1875-82), transformed NBR stock and introduced continuous braking with the Westinghouse system. (A E Glen Collection)

standards and on returning to Britain in 1863 determined to improve railway catering. They soon won company contracts including that for the NBR.

Travel on the NBR had its rules – from 1868 'no smoking' was revised when smoking compartments became available on carriages; however, if a smoker was caught in a 'non-smoker', a fine of 5s with 2s 6d expenses was levied. Non-payment of fares or travelling without a ticket continued to risk a fine or imprisonment.

By 1875, under careful management, the NBR

The Westinghouse air brake was installed widely and the pump was a recognisable feature on locomotives, as here on GNSR No.49 Gordon Highlander. (A E Glen)

was seeing its prospects improving, and a bold appointment was made for a new locomotive superintendent. This was Dugald Drummond, a forceful Scot who had proven competence in mechanical engineering and in railway operations. Many years before, he had worked with William Stroudley, first at Cowlairs on the E&GR, and later at the Highland Railway's Lochgorm Works in Inverness. By the 1870s, Stroudley was in charge of the London, Brighton & South Coast Railway where the Brighton line was noted for the fast running of locomotives. Coming from such a company, Drummond must have found the NBR depressing – it only had eight express locomotives. The need for new engines was urgent and Drummond rose to the challenge. His design of 4-4-0s for the difficult Waverley Route was outstanding. Soon the East Coast daytime expresses 'had been accelerated to the extent of a quarter of an hour over the Edinburgh & Glasgow line'.

The classes of Drummond locomotives – express, goods and tank engines – all had an identifiable style and many carried place names. This was useful publicity for the NBR in spreading information about places it served, but the names confused some passengers into thinking that these were train destinations. Locomotives came not only from Cowlairs but also from the Glasgow firms of Dübs and Neilson in a steady stream.

Continuous braking for passenger vehicles was a most desirable aim. In December 1876 Drummond held brake trials on the E&G route in the interests of improving safety. Two rival systems were tested – Smith's vacuum system and the Westinghouse air brake. Trains of eight carriages with a brake van at each end were marshalled for the test runs. With Smith's invention proving unreliable, Westinghouse was declared the winner. This decision resulted in a steam-operated air pump being mounted on locomotives, and its rhythmic thumping sound, when engines were stopped at stations, came to typify NBR trains for years. In 1877, the NBR was one of the first railways in Britain to fit continuous brakes to passenger carriages – a major advance in safety. The rival Caledonian Railway also adopted the Westinghouse system, but the Midland Railway, a close partner of the NBR, chose the vacuum variety, leading to 'dual fitting' of some rolling stock.

When carriages had no corridors or gangways (vestibule connections) at either end of the vehicle, tickets could not be checked in the course of a journey. Trains going into Queen Street station, stopped briefly at Cowlairs where there was a ticket platform for this purpose. This allowed ticket examiners to access compartments and punch tickets, a task that was estimated to add seven minutes to a journey. Once vestibuled carriages of corridor stock were introduced, tickets were inspected on board trains. Ticket platforms were then abandoned.

Meantime, there was a barrage of adverse criticism about Queen Street station's inconvenience, congestion and the hazards it presented for passengers – the city magistrates, the police and the public kept up complaints. As years of negative publicity were producing no betterment, in 1874 came a fresh attack. An astute Town Clerk of exceptional ability and experience had been appointed by Glasgow Corporation. This was James Marwick, an Orcadian, who had qualified as a lawyer, practised in Edinburgh, and had served the capital both as a Councillor and Town Clerk. In 1873, he was offered a generous salary to become the head of Glasgow's administration. Throughout his tenure, Marwick used his knowledge and influence not only to improve the quality of municipal services, such as lighting and water supply, but also to increase the city's status. A lasting achievement was his taking charge of moving the municipal offices from Trongate to George Square. On its east side, a magnificent City Chambers would be built – an endorsement of Glasgow's confidence and wealth. In such circumstances, it would be an embarrassment to have a city terminus in such wretched conditions as Queen Street so close to a civic icon. Marwick decried the NBR station as 'lacking any civic quality internally and any civic presence externally'. The station offered no welcome whatsoever to a great city.

The facilities at the other Glasgow termini were also generally inadequate – such as those at 'temporary' Buchanan Street and Dunlop Street stations, while old Bridge Street and South Side on the Clyde's south bank were poorly located for the city centre. At a Town Council meeting in July, the Lord Provost had stated, "No effort will be spared to bring about a reform in the present station arrangements in the city". When comment was made about the stations being a disgrace, the Lord Provost replied, "I think the North British is certainly the worst in the city".

Shortly, battle was joined. The offensive began with the Town Clerk's letter of 2 September 1873 to the directors of the NBR that referred to 'the insufficiency of Queen Street Station'. In 1863, the number of people using the station had been 1,575,000 but within ten years this had risen to over 3 million. With the opening or expansion of lines to the west served from Queen Street, the congestion had only got worse – lines to Helensburgh and to Balloch for Loch Lomond, together with the Milngavie branch – were producing many more passengers annually.

Before carriages had vestibule connections, trains stopped at ticket platforms outside principal stations. Such ticket checking was carried out at Cowlairs. (Mr Punch's Railway Book, Gutenberg)

At Queen Street, there were still only two narrow side platforms available for the passengers. Marwick described how passengers were crushed and jostled amid piles of luggage, while those forced to alight in the tunnel had to make their way into the station along a narrow ledge. 'When a long train is about to start, or two or more trains of ordinary length are to leave in quick succession, the utmost confusion and danger prevails'.

The NBR secretary, G B Wieland was instructed to reply – stating that the only accidents reported to him appeared to have been caused 'by want of reasonable care on the part of the passengers themselves'. This did not satisfy the Town Clerk who then took his concerns to the Board of Trade – on 6 November it raised the issue of 'increased accommodation' at the station. As the answer was probably unsatisfactory – it was well known that the NBR disliked spending money – and by 4 December the Board had instructed Captain Tyler of the Railway Inspectorate to investigate. On 18 December, the Captain's report was in the hands of the NBR directors. Tyler's key recommendation was that the goods yard should be given up in order to make a more commodious station with improved facilities for passengers, '*it was impossible to emphasise too strongly the urgent necessity that exists for removing the goods traffic elsewhere*' – but the report was ignored by the NBR.

The Town Clerk did not let matters rest and his letters continued. In January 1874, he was asking – probably tongue in cheek – 'whether the Company would illuminate the Queen Street Station on the occasion of the Duke of Edinburgh's marriage'. The Duke was Prince Alfred, a son of Queen Victoria who was to marry a Russian princess. The answer from the NBR

Sir James Marwick, the Town Clerk of Glasgow, was indefatigable in seeking improvements at Queen Street station and for the city. (Glasgow Museums)

51 goods covered vans and 25 goods guards vans. That year £35,000 was on deposit with the City of Glasgow Bank – the NBR was not hard up.

On 30 December Marwick had asked the Board of Trade to take further action, but the reply was disappointing, 'Your Corporation should understand distinctly that the Board of Trade has no power to make any order upon a Railway Company'. However, the case might be brought before a Royal Commission enquiring into railways in the cities.

A different tactic was now tried – Marwick contacted the Home Office. On 12 March 1875 the NBR directors had a letter from the Home Secretary Richard Cross intimating that 'in the event of any accident happening at Queen Street through the defective accommodation (there provided for the conduct of the traffic), the attention of the Lord Advocate as public prosecutor will be called to it'. (In Scotland, the Lord Advocate is the principal law officer). However, the Home Secretary professed himself powerless to intervene – and the Corporation found itself no better placed to get results than the NBR's many dissatisfied passengers. Claims over accidents at Queen Street kept coming – for instance, in June 1875 two ladies were awarded £25 and £7 10s for injuries sustained there, and a man received £4 4s. In October another lady received £80 for injuries suffered on 7 August. It is likely that women's long skirts made climbing in and out of the carriages on trains held in the tunnel especially hazardous.

was negative. Another letter on behalf of the Magistrates and Town Council again drawing attention to the 'insufficiency of accommodation' followed.

The NBR was spending some money. In January 1874 a turntable was ordered for Queen Street station at a cost of £301, and was charged to revenue. New rolling stock was being delivered – 38 horse boxes, 99 bar iron wagons,

The 1876 plan of Queen Street station prior to its reconstruction, showing dwelling houses lining North Hanover Street and the goods yard occupying as large an area as the passenger facilities. (National Records of Scotland)

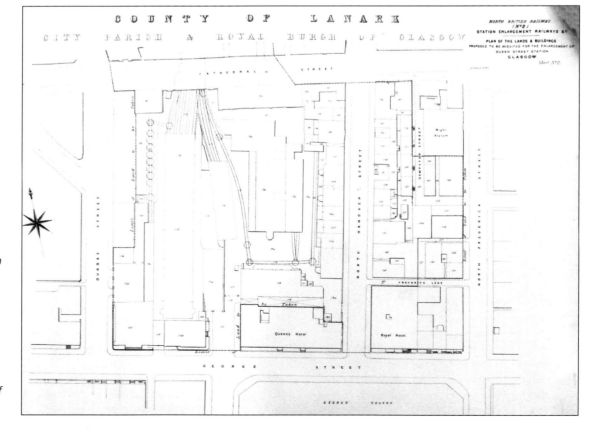

There was however some routine 'housekeeping' at the station. The cabstand was leased out in a money-making venture by the NBR and a new lessee had to be found. Then an enlargement of the Parcels Office was sanctioned – the parcels business was very profitable for the company. Yet nothing was done about a station 'bursting at the seams' – especially in July around the time of the Glasgow Fair.

By October 1875 Marwick employed a new strategy. In 1874 James Falshaw, a distinguished railway engineer but now retired, had become Lord Provost of Edinburgh. Among his many achievements had been overseeing the construction of the Lancaster & Carlisle Railway across Shap Summit in 1844. Such was Falshaw's repute that he was an advisor to the House of Commons on projects during the 'Railway Mania'. After moving to Stirling in 1845, he supervised the Caledonian Railway's line to Greenhill, and then the Scottish Central route completed to Perth in 1848. Another 'first' to which he contributed was the Inverness & Nairn Railway of 1855, but by 1861 his railway interests had been replaced by municipal politics. After settling in Edinburgh, he was soon a NBR director and the following year was a Baronet as Sir James Falshaw.

With Falshaw and Marwick having served on Edinburgh Town Council, they would be well acquainted. A committee consisting of Falshaw, and three other NBR directors was shortly appointed to examine plans for an enlarged Queen Street station and report. Parliamentary

Having retired from railway engineering, Sir James Falshaw served on Edinburgh Town Council and became Lord Provost. (Museums & Galleries, City of Edinburgh Council)

powers would have to be sought. However, the move was well timed as John Walker, subsequently acclaimed as the best general manager the NBR ever had, was now in charge.

In the Glasgow business community, there were some who saw a big investment opportunity arising around a new Queen Street station. In August 1874 challenging statements had come from James Keyden, a Glasgow solicitor.

The former site of the NBR's 7-storey granary adjacent to Cathedral Street and North Hanover Street to which the Corporation of Glasgow took strong objection. Latterly, the site was a car park and taxi rank.

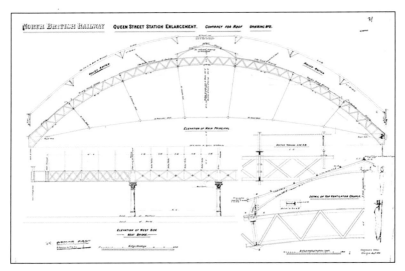

The drawing for the roof of the new train shed at Queen Street station. (Ask the Archivist, Network Rail)

'The inconvenience of the present Queen Street Station and its incline has long been keenly felt... in the height of summer, such multitudes present themselves ... that it became necessary to place the trains a very long way within the tunnel, and passengers were obliged to get in ... where the space between the carriages and the rock wall of the tunnel is very small indeed, and they could only get in with great difficulty or even danger...Public authorities are taking cognisance of this state of matters'.

Keyden then pointed out that the railway's natural outlet to Dumbartonshire (sic) was through the west end of Glasgow via Partick, an important suburb, and that a level line could be developed in that direction. An extensive station could be built adjoining Queen Street station, and another west at North Street in the Charing Cross district. A tunnel under Blythswood Hill would then join this line to the Stobcross Railway by the River Clyde. Journeys to Dumbarton, Helensburgh and the firth would be shortened. The incline would be given up and the Queen Street site – 'too short to admit proper platforms and other necessary conveniences for passenger traffic' would be redundant. 'Backers' would buy land for the project and pay £90,000 to the NBR on condition that the railway conveyed any surplus sites to them. This ambitious scheme was endorsed by the engineers Forman & McCall, who would become well known for construction works on Scottish lines, and who already had interests in the Stobcross and Whiteinch Railways.

The promoters of the Keyden scheme faced raising capital and drawing up a working and maintenance agreement – the NBR paying a toll of 2d per passenger for journeys of more than 5 miles to and from the refashioned Queen Street station; for journeys less than 5 miles, they would share 50-50. Trains using the incline would incur no charge. Although dabbling in land speculation involved 'a certain amount of risk', Keyden pursued a hard sales line – the

greatly enlarged Queen Street station could be got 'at almost no expense'. The moment must therefore be seized. He warned that new city and suburban stations were being developed by the Caledonian and the Glasgow & South Western Railways, both having plans for 'central stations in Glasgow at the expense of millions'. The North British must not be caught short.

A revised proposal was put on the table by December – these showed an 'elongation' of Queen Street station by opening out the tunnel mouth, a connection to College on the High Street and an underground station located near the west end of Sauchiehall Street. Although the scheme was presented as having outstanding merits, dealing with Queen Street station was the key problem, but the NBR board was determined that any works would only be done when the company itself was able to do these 'in house'.

There was then an interlude until January 1876 when another scheme was proposed by the civil engineer John Strain. He had considerable expertise in railway construction – the Callander & Oban route being a notable example. This had included the remodelling of Oban's sea front with an attractive promenade. He suggested that rail links between the College (now High Street) and Stobcross could be combined by realigning the Cowlairs tunnel 'to make the gradient workable without the rope'. A junction at Queen Street would allow all the NB lines to converge on a 'General Station' having its platforms at a level above George Street and George Square. The tunnel would then give access to a goods station to the north, but level with Cathedral Street. The Strain solution would have called for much tunnelling under city streets – both going west to Bath Street and east beneath John Street to reach High Street. His 'General Station' would have taken all the ground between Dundas Street and John Street, have six platforms, carriage and locomotive sidings and other facilities – under a roof similar to London's Victoria station. A long building three or four storeys high would front George Square where there would be a 'palatial hotel' with shops and offices at ground level. The 'deviation tunnel' proposed would have been a brute of 2,057yds (1880m), though the gradients could have been eased from 1 in 70 to 1 in 250.

The raising of £1.4m for this ambitious project, by issuing preference stock, was tried but was unsuccessful – the NBR's financial debacle of 1866 had not been forgotten. For the NBR directorate, Walker's response – to what must have seemed a flight of fancy – was polite, *'the Board are disinclined to incur ... the enormous expense in carrying out any of the larger schemes'.* (In February 1877, when the directors had finally settled on an 'in house' solution, they then offered Strain a free pass on the NBR for a year).

The cumulative effect of the criticism of Queen Street station, and the well publicised solutions, eventually provoked action. On 10 August 1876, a report was at last submitted to the NBR board about an 'in house' plan and this was approved. In September, a proposed meeting would be held with Glasgow Corporation when three of the directors, led by Sir James Falshaw, would attend. The solution would be based on 'Mr Carswell's plan'. James Carswell was a senior engineer with the NBR. He had experience both in iron founding through his family background, and in railways through his work with the Monkland Railway and the E&GR. He would prove an expert in malleable iron construction, as the new train shed at Queen Street would show.

On 9 November 1876 news came that Parliamentary powers had been obtained for re-modelling the station. The Act received Royal Assent on 17 May 1877 and authorised the company 'to enlarge their Queen Street Station in Glasgow... to acquire additional lands and to stop up certain streets in Glasgow', among a variety of other works. The fact that the rival Caledonian Railway had got permission in 1875 to bridge the Clyde – hence its Central Station with eight platforms was on its way – must have concentrated NBR minds. It was soon reported that properties in Cathedral Street and Holmhead Street had been acquired for an outlay of £60,000. At High Street, with a view to an improved station replacing the 'College' facilities, there were further acquisitions costing in excess of £48,000. When tenders were invited for ironwork and mason work, the ironwork prices varied from £11,000 to £17,000 and the mason work from £23,000 to £51,000. On 29 November 1877 there was an offer from James Young & Sons, an experienced firm of Edinburgh contractors, for 'the works of enlargement' amounting to £34,414 5s 7d, the contractor paying £3,500 for materials recovered from buildings taken down and including carting rubble to College – wagons then took this by rail to widen the Coatbridge line. Masonry would be re-used in the project. Young agreed to complete the work by 20 September 1878 when a bonus of £500 would be earned.

In January 1878 a new grain store was under discussion. The Town Council deplored the locating of this 7-storey structure at Queen Street. The traffic of horse and carts did not enhance the ambience of George Square, and there was a downside to cleanliness in city streets through spilt grain and horse droppings.

To put an ambitious station project on the restricted site – being mindful of the former quarry there – caused problems. There was damage to property with requests for

compensation, and inconvenience when the NBR stables in North Hanover Street had to be moved. Indeed, in May, the NBR was proposing to build across North Hanover Street and onto land owned by Glen's Institution (later known as Allan Glen's School). This had been established in 1853 for the sons of tradesmen in Glasgow's East End, and its trustees were hoping to expand their premises. It soon became likely that the NBR would have to spend £50,000 on property purchases and legal fees in order to close up North Hanover Street – a sum that warned the company off the move. In July came offers for the grain store works varying from £9,321 to £11,700, covering 'Digger and Mason Works', 'Carpenter, Joiner & Ironmongery', and 'Slater and Plumber Works'. An offer of £10,300 was accepted.

James Carswell's plan for the station roof survives. In June 1878, contractors were invited 'with specifications prepared immediately and tenders thereafter advertised' based on his design. In September, P&W MacLellan made an offer to build the structure for the new train shed of malleable iron and glass. From humble beginnings in 1805 at a hardware shop in Glasgow's Trongate, MacLellans had risen to prominence, first in manufacturing a variety of iron goods, including nuts, bolts and rivets for

The Old College site in the High Street was earmarked for railway use and was a temporary station in the latter 1870s. (The Annan Collection)

Clyde shipbuilders. Within a few years, they were constructing iron bridges, thus moving into structural engineering. Their offer for the train shed roof amounted to £17,800, but shortly the company was prepared to accept £17,500. (A key proposal was dispensing with 'Rendle's Patent System of Glazing' – probably to save costs. The system did not require putty and was widely used at railway stations where it was said to be undamaged by the passage of express trains. It had also been tried at cabstands at the new St Enoch station).

The grain store also advanced – this L-shaped granary was likely to cost £10,000 to £11,751 and have four storey facades at street level. The NBR stables in North Hanover Street now had to be pulled down, but these housed 104 horses; a few were employed in shunting vehicles in the goods yard while others collected or delivered merchandise, 'luggage' and other loads on behalf of the company in the city. Traffic in hay was considerable – the outlays per horse, then 1s 5d per week, were regularly reported at directors' meetings.

Just when the NBR seemed more confident about spending money – and with the reconstruction at Queen Street station getting into its stride – came the news on 2 October 1878 of the collapse of the City of Glasgow Bank. Established in 1839 it appealed to small investors attracted by its high interest rates on their deposits. In 1857, it had survived a banking crisis when business had been suspended. Despite this setback, it re-opened and continued to trade offering big dividends of 9 to 12 per cent to investors. Evening openings were helpful to shopkeepers and traders, but from November 1877 there were misgivings about the bank's speculations. Net liabilities of £6m were concealed by false reports and by accountancy aimed at bolstering its share price. When the crisis broke, all but 254 of the bank's 1,200 shareholders were ruined. Without limited liability many Glasgow businesses failed and families became bankrupt. The bank's directors were arrested and tried. The episode highlighted the need for limited liability. The NBR had some £250,000 invested in the bank, but they also had a loan on which the liquidators looked for

interest. Reductions in wages and salaries of 5 to 10 per cent ensued with the directors taking a 15 per cent cut in their recompense. (In the latter 1880s, the NBR had to be content with the liquidators paying ¾ per cent interest on their investment).

The works at Queen Street began early in 1878 with the removal of the lower tunnel portion in 30ft sections, posing 'great difficulty as the old stone arches ... were blown up with dynamite and powder'. The work was mainly on Sundays – soon 170 yds (155m) was cleared, with excavated material being taken by rail to double the Shettleston-Parkhead line. The blasting may have led to the mouth of the Queen Street tunnel collapsing on 17 August 1879:–

'The operations for the enlargement of the NBR station at Queen Street have suddenly come to a temporary stop through the subsidence of a large portion of the tunnel discovered at 10pm on Sunday night when all traffic was suspended ...the fall extended to some 70ft ...a mass of stone and earth... efforts were made from both ends and will take several days to clear. Via Cowlairs, traffic for Edinburgh, Helensburgh and branches will be from College station'.

– The Glasgow Evening Advertiser

Some trains of empty stock were trapped at Queen Street. Passengers were conveyed by omnibuses from Dundas Street to College station for their onward journeys and a new station at High Street was delayed for a year. The tunnel was reopened on 27 August with its mouth now north of Cathedral Street. The Board of Trade appointed Major-General Hutchinson to investigate 'the new works at Queen Street Station' and report. The civil engineers Simpson & Wilson, who would shortly be responsible for the Glasgow City & District Railway, also produced a report– both being read to directors on 12 September.

Massive retaining walls – up to 13 feet thick to withstand ground pressure from the forced earth of the old quarry – were constructed at the tunnel mouth where the extension was 153yds (140m). Sandstone was also quarried for masonry. The new bridge at Cathedral Street by Smith & Wilson came from their Bellahouston Iron Works and was supported on 30ft piles plus a large bed of concrete. In November came reports of further damage to property at Holmhead Street for which compensation of £6,500 was asked – legal advice was to acquire it, but the NBR was now running out of such options.

By 1878 passenger comfort on the NBR had at last received attention – probably a Midland Railway effect – when most second class

Top: *The new train shed of malleable iron, with its roof clad in glass and timber, with steel tie rods to give additional support, was constructed by P&W MacLellan. The centre 'roads' between platforms allowed trains to be stored in the station. (Strathclyde Regional Archives)*

Left: *The widened approach at the Cowlairs tunnel seen when the retaining walls were stone cleaned in 1983, prior to air space being taken by Buchanan Galleries for a pedestrian bridge to a large car park. (J L Stevenson)*

Right: *One of twenty cast iron Corinthian columns that support the train shed roof. Several were encased in bricks and tiles in the 1970s but have now been uncovered.*

carriages became thirds. Batches of new carriages were also designed by Drummond – first and third class examples being exhibited in Edinburgh. These were thought 'traditional' rather than innovative, and there were questions over the safe use of 'gasoline' rather than oil lamps for lighting the vehicles. The Board of Trade was now insisting on continuous footboards along the length of carriages in the interests of employee safety when ticket checking on non-vestibuled vehicles.

In December 1879, the Tay Bridge, the new NBR link through Fife to the north, was destroyed in a winter storm taking a passenger train with it. This was a national tragedy posing serious questions about engineering, about wind strength and about the competence of the

NBR directors to run a railway safely.

Yet in Glasgow by 1880, passengers at Queen Street station could wonder at the new train shed, 'a handsome edifice' flooded with light. Its glazed tied arch, over 78ft (16m) in height, supported laterally on Corinthian columns in cast iron, had taken shape, and now enclosed a space of 450ft (137m) by 250ft (76m) with seven platforms. James Carswell, the NBR engineer, had a mentor in William Barlow, the distinguished engineer and associate of George Stephenson. With Barlow's wide experience in railways, he was appointed to lead the Midland Railway's extension from Bedford to London in 1862. He had designed St Pancras station with a train shed roof having a clear span of 240ft, then the largest in the world. After 1876 when the

The north side of Queen Street station from the Cathedral Street bridge shows the train shed, looking west.

The view looking south shows the extent of the train shed roof stretching towards West George Street.

Settle & Carlisle line opened and the MR became a partner for the NBR over the Waverley Route, the relationship between the companies became close. Barlow investigated the use of steel, and at Queen Street the malleable iron latticework of the roof has steel tie rods supported by steel hangers. The roof was covered with glass, timber and slates. A plaque high on the south façade records P&W McLellan's craftsmanship at their Clutha Works at Kinning Park and carries the date 1881.

When the works at Queen Street were completed, the passenger station's extent had almost doubled from just 7,900 (6605m²) to 15,560 sq yd (13,010m²). The two old platforms

had been replaced by seven new ones amounting to 6,560 sq yd (5485m²), with durable 'granolithic' surfaces instead of timber. There was a cabstand on the east side and sidings for some 170 carriages. A signal box on a gantry spanning the lines at the station's throat had 60 levers controlling the points and signals. It was soon announced that bullhead rail, made of steel at 84lbs per yard, would be laid in the station and tunnel – the directors relieved that there was no need to alter the chairs.

There were some reservations about the new station – the contracts had not covered the booking and general offices, tasks that would be deferred indefinitely:–

'until this improvement is carried out, it is impossible to say that the principal Glasgow terminus of the NBR is all that it should be'. – The Glasgow Herald

James Carswell as an engineer had a salary of £600 per annum, but he received £1,000 for the preparation of plans for 'the rearrangement and enlargement of Queen Street Station' (a sum equivalent to £120,000 in 2020). There was also a payment of £1,000 to 'Mr Barlow' – for 'plan of restoration', clearly recompense for his input to the station improvements. Both engineers would soon be involved in the Forth Bridge project in which James Carswell would play a key role in the design of the approach viaducts.

The plaque on the cast iron bridge is for the builders Smith & Naysmith of Bellahouston Ironworks, Glasgow.

Chapter 4

The Innovative 1880s

The first use of electricity in the City of Glasgow was in 1879 at a railway station – the newly opened and impressive St Enoch of the Glasgow & South Western Railway where the great arch of its train shed was lit by six arc lamps. The power supply was generated specifically for station use and the North British Railway had to catch up. Hitherto, stations and most of the city had been lit by coal gas.

Two rival systems were on offer – from Crompton or from Brush. R E B Crompton was a British electrical engineer and inventor. In 1878, Crompton & Company was formed to manufacture and install his design of lamps. This was so successful that he was soon making a rival's light bulbs under licence. By 1881 the Crompton range covered complete electrical systems from dynamos to switchgear and he had installed lights at such prestigious locations as King's Cross station and Windsor Castle. Soon he was supplying electrical equipment throughout the British Empire.

The other manufacturer was Charles F Brush, an American engineer and inventor. In 1879, the Brush Electric Light Corporation was established based on Brush developments. Many American and Canadian cities invested in Brush lighting. On moving to Britain, Brush set up business in Loughborough as 'Brush Electrical Engineering Co Ltd' but this was sold to Thomson-Houston in 1889.

By June 1880 the 'expediency' of having electric light at Queen Street station caused a

The 1880s saw innovations such as the 'speaking telegraph', soon known as the telephone invented by Alexander Graham Bell that would transform railway communications. (Wikipedia)

committee of directors to 'enquire and report'. On 9 September, this group met to discuss electric lighting, and by 21 October, an arrangement had been made with 'Mr Crompton, London, through agents, Messrs Henry Bennett & Company of Glasgow', to fit it up lights, 'experimentally', the cost to the NBR being 4s an hour 'when the lights burn'. The power would be produced using a coal-fired boiler to provide steam to drive a dynamo, and thus generate electricity. A further 6 months trial was agreed in June 1881. There had also been an agreement to light Waverley station. By July, 'Swan's Incandescent Electric Lamps' were illuminating the goods shed at Queen Street and would soon be used in the booking and other offices.

In December 1881, a letter from R E Crompton offered electric lighting for Queen

Seen among the advertisements at Queen Street station in the 1890s was this NBR 0-4-2T locomotive No.1080, much rebuilt and dating from 1866. (Postcard & Covers/Photomatic)

Weighing machines and other 'penny-in-the-slot' delights were soon installed at railway stations; weighing machines appeared at Queen Street station in 1885. (Mr Punch's Railway Book, Gutenberg)

Street at £400 for 12 months, with the NBR supplying the coal. Crompton then tried to persuade the railway company to buy the plant for £1,200 after a year's use – if the lights continued to give satisfaction. Negotiations began and he offered to accept £360 plus free coal and to install three extra lights. Meanwhile, the Brush Company at Waverley station was offering lighting for £504, plus free coal, and the general manager was instructed to arrange 'better terms'. The result was a two-year contact from May 1882 with 'the Scottish Brush Electric Light & Power Co Ltd'.

Crompton continued at Queen Street on annual contracts but by 1883 the general manager was told to purchase 'on the best possible terms' the electricity plant at Queen Street now operated by the Swan Electric Light Co Ltd.

Safety on the railway at Queen Street was improved in 1880 when a block telegraph cabin was installed at the north end of the Cowlairs tunnel for £120. For telegraph messages, there was a stand off as the GPO, then in charge, shut

Enamel signs ushered in an advertising revolution, with railway companies receiving rent for displaying them; this is a well covered Polmont station. (J L Stevenson Collection)

down the NBR Glasgow stations for public use. It had offered 1d per message but the former rate had been 3d and the NBR board would not budge. However, permission was given to the GPO to erect a 'letter pillar box' at Queen Street 'at the pleasure of the directors'.

Communications were advancing and the Edison Telephone Company was permitted to fix eight wires to NBR property in Dundas Street – at 3 months notice with a rent of one shilling per wire per annum. By August 1884, the extension of the 'speaking telegraph' to Aberfoyle at a cost of £120 was also permitted and shortly 'telephonic communication between Perth and Glasgow stations' would be possible. Soon an arrangement was made with the National Telephone Company to erect poles and wires along stretches of the railway.

While the economy was not perceived as buoyant, there was a renewal of advertising for five years with 'English & Scotch Advertising Company' at £1,070 per annum, an increase of £70. From the 1870s, enamel signs were being displayed at railway sites – on stations, walls and fences. Enamel was both colourful and durable, being 'impervious to the effects of weather, resisting vandalism and being easy to wipe clean', advantages that appealed to railway companies. The NBR had no hesitation in having masonry walls covered with such advertisements – and being paid rent to do so. The showy designs helped to brighten the smoke-stained interiors of stations such as Queen Street. Now the places where such signs were fixed show as filled holes in the stonework.

The basis for the signs was sheet iron to which metal oxides and glass were applied. While Birmingham manufacturers were pioneers, the Falkirk Iron Company was a major Scottish producer. The signs became part of an advertising revolution that took many products from being 'local' to being known and used nationwide. From biscuits and beverages, ointments and tonics to soap and washing powders, cigarettes and ink, marketing quickly advanced. Although the Temperance Movement was active, and the NBR had a Temperance Society, advertisements for alcohol, whether ales, wines or whiskies were common at its stations, including Queen Street. Surviving signs are now sought after as 'collectables'.

As traffic had been increasing, there were bonuses for some managers. Queen Street station was busy, and with reports of luggage going missing, £500 was spent on improving the 'storage accommodation and cloakrooms'. But the terminus had a continuing weakness – the Cowlairs Incline with its wire rope haulage, an installation of November 1884 failing in June 1885. A new wire rope from Haggie Brothers, Gateshead cost £77 17s per ton but came with a

An engine shed at Cowlairs supplied the locomotives for Queen Street trains. The tall chimney for the Engine House on the incline is seen far left. (NBRSG Archive)

guarantee of 10 months.

That year the NBR directors received a letter from the Automatic Weighing Machine Company offering to install its equipment at NBR stations. In Britain, 'penny in the slot machines' were the invention of Percival Everett, a Norfolk man who patented them. As an amusement, they were an immediate success and were soon followed by other devices. Weighing machines were imitated by an offer to install 'strength testing' devices at stations. Vending machines that could supply small objects of regular size were soon produced, and in 1887 the 'Sweetmeat Automatic Delivery Company' was set up by Everett. Shortly, the first 'penny in the slot' machines dispensing Cadbury's or Nestle's chocolate bars appeared. Selling cigarettes and matches followed and amusement and vending machines were installed around the concourse at Queen Street station. The NBR received rent but soon began looking for 10 per cent of the takings. Railway stations with footfalls of thousands – where passengers might have time on their hands – were ideal sites for such machines.

In 1889 an enquiry from Cumming Patents Ltd of Edinburgh was for an 'exhibition' for three months of six 'Automatic Photographic Delivery Machines', six to be placed at Queen Street and six at Waverley, for the sum of £18. These would prove to be very popular. By 1892 the Scottish Automatic Supply Company was requesting the installation of 'Grip, Twist and Pistol' machines at stations. They also asked to place a number – not exceeding 100 – of small sweetmeat machines at NBR stations at a rental of 10s (50p) a year for each. By 1901, 'sweetmeat' machines and other 'amusements' could be seen in almost all of Britain's 7,000 railway stations, plus public houses, hotels and resorts.

Increasingly, railway stations had become hubs, both for those who were travelling and for the general public – places to buy newspapers, confectionery or tobacco from kiosks, to have shoes polished by 'shoe blacks', to see the passenger throngs and view the activity on the railway, especially if new locomotives or coaches were introduced. There was also the opportunity to go to the 'Refreshment Rooms' where 'alcoholic beverages' could be bought. In June 1880 there was an agreement to continue with the lease for these premises with Spiers & Pond, the partnership of repute that had seen a business opportunity by improving catering on railways. By 1873 they managed over 100 railway refreshment rooms for nine companies, had built restaurants in association with theatres and owned several hotels. They also provided hampers for passengers in transit. The rental agreement with Spiers & Pond was for £2,250 per annum to cover both Queen Street and Waverley. As their facilities – with their attractive barmaids – appeared to prosper, the NBR was considering a takeover.

An additional excitement at Queen Street was to watch the brakemen with their special wagons that brought trains down the incline into the station, but 'buffer stop' collisions featured regularly in the press – in January 1883, there was another when a train ran 'violently against the stationary buffers at Queen Street'. Compensation for accidents mounted and a total of £1,105 was quoted for episodes at Queen Street and £2,420 at Cowlairs that may also have covered works injuries; yet the NBR board refused to donate to St Andrews Ambulance Society. It would however send out leaflets for the Railway Benevolent Society and place 'contribution boxes' for the Royal National Lifeboat Institute on NBR steamers.

Seen on the right at Cowlairs is the locomotive that hauled the train opening the Forth Bridge in March 1890 when new routes became operable from Queen Street. (National Records of Scotland)

In November 1883 the intention to purchase a piece of ground for an engine shed at Eastfield was announced. Hitherto, the NBR had made do with a portion of Cowlairs Works for the engines that serviced Queen Street trains. The directors had their eyes on 5,302 sq yds (5448m²) 'provided it can be obtained at a reasonable price'. There were worries about the presence of coal and the compensation to be paid for the use of land that contained it.

There was growing pressure to make railway services available in the West End of Glasgow. In 1881 a petition was sent to the NBR board on behalf of ' Merchants, Bankers, Manufacturers and others' resident in Kelvinside, Hillhead and Partick for the 'Glasgow City and Dumbartonshire Railway'. Hitherto railway schemes had 'all been carried southward and eastward, leaving 'the great and populous district in the west ... unprovided with railway accommodation'. There were over 700 signatories on the petition. For a bold scheme from Hyndland, then tunnelling under Hillhead and Garnethill before swinging NE to avoid Cowlairs, the engineers would be Formans & McCall.

The residents in Glasgow's West End had a point. When lines were to be developed towards the city along the north bank of the Clyde, it was soon discovered that much of the 'western approaches' was already built up. The solution was to circumvent such areas by swinging round the city's northern perimeter. This was the route taken by the independently promoted Glasgow, Dumbarton & Helensburgh Railway that opened its line in 1858. At the outset, the only intermediate station between its junction with the E&GR at Cowlairs and Dalmuir was at Maryhill, then a canal-side village. On reaching Cowlairs, the line dropped down the incline to Queen Street and the GD&HR was absorbed by the E&GR in 1862.

The NBR solution to the 'disconnection' with the city's west was the Glasgow City & District Railway, a major investment for which the NBR

was a sponsor, though a separate company delivered the line. Most of the finance came from the Bairds of Gartsherrie, wealthy ironmasters and major shareholders in the NBR. It was a challenging project for its engineers and contractors and only the fourth underground railway in Britain. In August 1882 its prospectus was issued to NBR shareholders. On paper, 'Railway No 1' was a short line just 2.365 miles (3.8km) long, running east-west, principally below the city, connecting existing lines that terminated at College station on the east. 'Railway No 2' was a spur connecting the existing Stobcross branch at Finnieston with the Helensburgh line, both 'ends' of the underground railway being some distance from the city centre. When fulfilled, the project would enable trains from Airdrie, Coatbridge and Hamilton to be brought into an underground station at Queen Street; from there, Helensburgh and Vale of Leven services could be run over the Stobcross branch through Partick, thus relieving haulage on the Cowlairs Incline. A circular and completing link would pass through Bellgrove, Springburn, Maryhill and a station at Great Western Road to reach Partick.

After obtaining the sanction of Parliament in 1882, two contracts were let by the GC&DR for the three tunnelling works on the new line. The contract for High Street tunnel, and the portion from West Campbell Street to College went to Charles Brand & Son, and the western portion from Stobcross to West Campbell Street to James Young & Son, Edinburgh. For works at Finnieston, Hugh Kennedy & Sons of Partick were employed. Four bridges were also required on the line. The engineers for the project were Simpson & Wilson.

The addition of Finnieston brought the NBR into discussions with the Caledonian Railway. The NBR branch to Finnieston opened in 1874 and the CR had running powers over it, therefore its interests had to be considered when a Finnieston station on the G&CDR was being designed. (The CR's Glasgow Central Railway of 1894 would see another station opened at Finnieston).

The work on the GC&DR began in March 1883 and turned much of central Glasgow into a construction site for four years. After bore hole investigations, by May, there was activity at nine points with shafts being sunk for tunnels, trenches dug and retaining walls being built. The 'very varied character' of the geology under Glasgow was perplexing – ranging from sandstone and shale, to boulder clay, mud and running sand – the latter was an unwelcome feature and the worst material to handle. Going west the alignment of the GC&DR followed West Regent Street. When tunnelling under Hope Street, there was a sudden transition from firm boulder clay to soft shale owing to the presence of a large fault and subsidence resulted with buildings on both sides of the street being affected, 'considerable sums having to be paid for structural damage'.

From Wellington Street, the tunnel continued under Blythswood Hill towards Charing Cross. There a wider tunnel 102yd (93m) in length was formed to accommodate a station. In June 1884, the west half of Elmbank Crescent had to be removed. This curving terrace of town houses was built prior to the 1860s in a simple Georgian style and overlooked gardens. (Only one of the original properties now stands on the south side as a Quakers' Meeting House). Work soon began on the retaining walls at the station site. Another awkward location was St Vincent Crescent with its tenement flats and basements where a property had to be taken down – running sand again giving the engineers' concerns. In areas of housing, piling was only done by day, with no night shifts to avoid disturbing residents.

At Kent Road, to prevent the collapse of the tall tenement housing on its flanks, when running sand was encountered and cracks appeared in walls, sheet piling was driven on both sides of the street. A method was devised based on the principle that dry sand occupied the same volume as wet sand – once the water was completely drained from it. This technique for coping with running sand would be acknowledged as 'novel'. Kent Road was then excavated to the level of the tunnel arch when concreting of the arch could take place. It all took time – to allow drainage of the water, but retain the sand. Step by step, cavities were made for the tunnel's sidewalls and then filled with concrete while an invert was then poured to carry the formation. The result was basically a concrete tube 700yds (640m) long to contain the railway. With sewers and drains tapped, a major drain was constructed and a siphon installed to take water to the Clyde.

Concrete was used extensively on the GC&DR, and both concreting and the brick lining of the tunnels was done continuously. Spoil from the shafts, typically driven at street intersections, was carted to Stobcross, tipped into railway wagons and taken to make up banking on the branch from Partick to Hyndland. The Hyndland branch was an addition to the programme for the GC&DR, and possibly a reaction to the 'Glasgow City and Dumbartonshire Railway' petition from West End citizens.

The city centre presented severe construction difficulties. All the streets were busy thoroughfares, several being where the Corporation's horse trams plied and interruption had to be minimised:–

'To get across Renfield Street, piles were driven between the tramway rails during the night; the

The only original property standing at Elmbank Crescent is now a Quaker Meeting House.

causeway and rails were lifted on a Sunday, and then supported on timbers resting on the piles...the surface being restored on a following Sunday'. – Robert Simpson in Inst.Eng.&Ship.Scot.Proc. Vol 31, 1887-88

The piles were 30ft (9m) long, in three pieces and were driven home by a crane.

From West Nile Street to Buchanan Street the tunnel widened to 35ft (10.6m) for access to the new Low Level station at Queen Street; here a 'cut and cover' method through rock could be used, but the commercial buildings adjacent had to be underpinned. The Queen Street site itself was mixture of sandstone and 'forced material' from the old quarry.

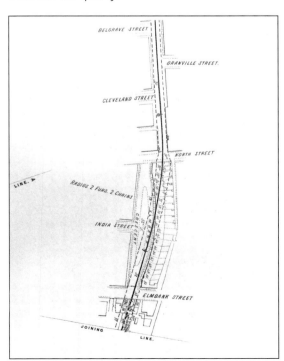

A plan for the original Charing Cross station on the Glasgow & City District Railway that became a battleground over air pollution. (National Records of Scotland)

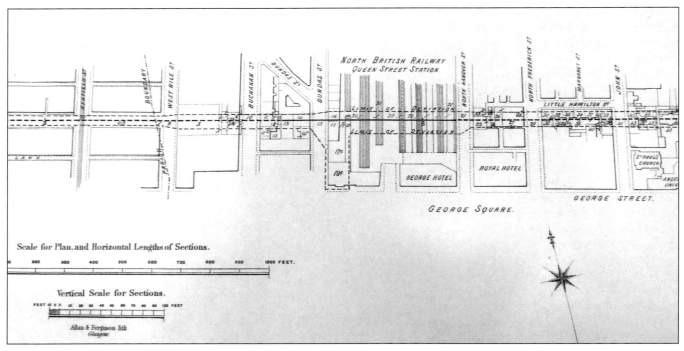

The plan for the G&CDR's access beneath Queen Street station caused problems in Central Glasgow. (National Records of Scotland)

In July 1883, on Brand's contract for the east section, three shafts were sunk for tunnelling as 75 per cent of its length was through sandstone, and between George Street and High Street, 'cut and cover' was thought possible and straightforward. One shaft was located at a site well known to Glaswegians – in Hengler's Circus, a popular entertainment venue famous for its equestrian displays – it shortly moved away to Sauchiehall Street. However, on the east side of George Street, the rock – with a thin cover of boulder clay – dipped into a deep glacial valley filled with soft wet mud. There were now unexpected difficulties – the site was so wet that 'men always had to stand on boards' to work. As the timber piles could not reach rock, pairs of brick caissons, well weighted down, were sunk until firm ground was reached. Once the caissons were filled with concrete, the tunnel was constructed on top of them. It was slow going – less than a yard (1m) a month compared with 6.5yd (6m) when tunnelling through rock and 12yd (11m) in 'cut and cover'. The subsidence in the area was also 'very considerable', all the houses between Frederick Street and George Street having to be taken down.

At the peak of construction, 22 tunnelling faces were in action. The extent of the tunnels was 2,600yds (2377m) of which 1,050yds (960m) was constructed by the 'cut and cover' method. There was an advantage for the city in such profound engineering – the Corporation got the benefit of massively improved drainage and sewerage. Going west the larger drains totalled 86, with a 4ft (1.2m) diameter drain inserted 8ft (2.4m) beneath the rails near Charing Cross, and the West Nile Street drain well below the formation. It was discovered that some sewers

had been cut in solid rock, some lay in arches of old brickwork, while other main drains crossed the railway – at Buchanan Street and High Street, a malleable iron trough lined with brick did so.

Probably the most testing location was the making of Queen Street Low Level station. It was arranged 'nearly at right angles to the high level station and 18ft (5.4m) below it'. The work was done in bays, those in the goods yard each having a loading table with a roadway on the east side, while in the passenger station half a platform and the line of rails beside it was the allocation. The station was divided into strips each 45ft (13.7m) in length and 110ft (33.5m) in width – the latter corresponding with the width of the low level station. In all, there were eleven bays with the work taking two years to complete. Remarkably, it was accomplished without interrupting the traffic in the High Level station.

To form the Low Level station, trenches were excavated for abutments and retaining walls in the High Level with pits made for the centre support columns; the bases for these were blocks of concrete 2ft (0.6m) thick with a granite block on top to form the sole. Girders with a span of 48ft (14.6m) were then put across and once the iron flooring was complete, the platform and rails could be restored at the High Level. Spoil was taken from below by rail to College (later High Street) that was transformed into a through station.

A major exercise was to insert the girders under the large cast iron columns supporting the roof of the train shed. The first stage saw four 12in (0.30m) piles driven down – one at each corner of the foundation on which the column stood. When these piles reached 'hard', an iron superstructure of beams and angle irons was erected around the column. Hydraulic jacks

The Low Level station in 2019 looking west from Platform 9 with the pillars supporting the High Level station.

on the superstructure gave support, 'The column was thus left hanging in the air, and in this position it was easily cut and the girder placed underneath'. Impressive though the insertion of the Low Level station might be, the NBR board disliked the projecting girders that appeared in the High Level station. (These have been recently strengthened and can be seen between platforms 2 and 3, 4 and 5).

In February 1886, with the GC&DR close to completion, Major-General Hutchinson inspected the railway. He noted the projecting girders at the High Level station but left the NBR general manager to sort matters out. Earlier there had been an inspection of the short Hyndland branch and the hypothetical Great Western Road station by the directors – this latter site would become 'Anniesland' in 1931.

The train service and fares, including season ticket rates were now considered. With the GC&DR nominally independent, a meeting had taken place with the NBR board on 1 March and negotiations for amalgamation were continued.

Meantime, it was proposed that that a NBR tank engine would be altered to a condensing locomotive as an experiment. Condensing systems were first used in 1864 on locomotives for London's Metropolitan Railway; steam was returned through piping to the cold water in the side tanks with the intention that it would be condensed there, thus reducing steam exhaust in tunnels. The method was not entirely successful and there is no evidence that any NBR engine was so fitted. The early notion that locomotives would 'consume their own smoke' had long since been disproved – condensing

At the High Level station, girders have been recently strengthened, showing where the G&CDR tracks lie below.

The G&CDR used existing NBR locomotives. These Drummond 4-4-0 tank engines of 1879 built by Neilson with 6ft coupled wheels had a name for fast running on the Helensburgh trains. (Euan Crawford)

systems did nothing to reduce smoke. No goods trains were permitted on the low level line to help minimise steam and smoke.

The GC&DR opened on 15 March 1886 when it was reported that the trains kept excellent time, were well filled with passengers and would run daily until eleven o'clock at night. Queen Street Low Level had four platforms – two on either side of a large island – and designated A, B, C and D to prevent confusion with the High Level numbers. From street level, the Low Level platforms were reached by steep stairs but hydraulic hoists were installed for luggage and parcels.

The GC&DR had just opened when on 18 March there was a collision outside Finnieston tunnel. A passenger train to Helensburgh was standing in Finnieston station when a train from Queen Street for Maryhill emerged from the tunnel. A signal box stood close to the tunnel mouth but neither the signalman nor the engine driver could see the signal owing to the 'thick atmosphere'. As the train was slowing up, its force was not great but it ran into the back of the Helensburgh train where several passengers were severely shaken by the impact, some sustaining cuts and bruises. There was practically no damage to the rolling stock or

Carriages on the line were typically NBR third class compartment stock. (NBRSG Archive)

track, but it was adverse publicity for the new line. That same day there was a derailment following a collision with goods trains at Bellgrove.

When the Board of Trade report from Major-General Hutchinson about Finnieston appeared, the main recommendation was to shift the signal box away from the tunnel mouth to the 'down end' of the station and put disc signals at eye level in the tunnel. He was assured that the NBR was 'making alterations in the engines that habitually work trains on the G&CDR as will permit of their steam being condensed in the tunnels'.

What were those engines? They were tank engines principally of two types – 0-4-4T and 0-6-0T locomotives, both of Drummond design. Among the former were ones with 6ft driving wheels that were associated with Helensburgh trains where long stretches of track were fairly level and fast running was possible. From 1882, and the appointment of Matthew Holmes as Locomotive Superintendent, they had lost the names of places served by the NBR that they had once carried. The other 0-4-4Ts had smaller wheels, as had the 0-6-0Ts but both classes were versatile and suitable for freight or passenger duties. There were no new engines for the underground railway. For coaching stock, it was the same – passengers had to endure the shaking, rattling discomfort of the NBR's six wheelers of which many complained. Workmen's trains might consist of four wheelers that had seen many years of hard use.

Did the NBR board pay any attention to such protests? After the GC&DR opened, a local committee at Milngavie asked for an extra train back from Glasgow at '5.20 or 5.30'.This was agreed, but a reduction in fares for season tickets was refused.

The NBR's intention to take over the G&CDR was not immediate, and by August the general manager was left to arrange terms for the amalgamation. At Stobcross, the GC&DR had surplus land for sale and it offered to convey this to the NBR and CR companies for £14,781 16s – the price paid for it, with 18 months interest at 5 per cent. It was willing 'to treat' for this with the CR, or 'exclusively' with the NBR. The branch to Knightswood was opened that month, but any further expansion of the system was put on hold, an extension from Yorkhill to Hillhead being declined.

The halfmile long branch to Hyndland station had also opened on 15 March 1883. This West End terminus soon had 46 trains each way per day, serving Coatbridge and Airdrie, plus the Hamilton lines, and among the total were 16 trains to and from Edinburgh. The City of Glasgow Union Railway, in which the NBR had a share with the G&SWR, now gave the possibility of a circular route from Queen Street Low Level out and back via Maryhill. Although the CGU's purpose was basically to handle goods traffic, it had passenger potential, and by 1887 three new stations were opened on it at Springburn, Barnhill and Garngad. The Low Level also had trains to Dumbarton, Balloch and Helensburgh, affording much needed relief to the High Level station.

These developments highlighted the significance of the new Low Level station that gave the NBR two major stations on one 'city centre' site, thanks to the ingenious engineering of Scotland's first underground railway. The opening even had its consequences for the letting of the cab stance at Queen Street – it was let to 'Messrs Lawson' at £250, but only for a year pending the opening of the GC&DR. The underground line had the potential to double station activity and thus the number of hires – with the possibility of an increased rental for the NBR.

The problem of lighting carriages in the dark tunnels was soon raised, the services being considered 'unsuitable for females'. Initially oil lamps on the tunnel walls were tried, but were soon abandoned in favour of an electrical system. The NBR board authorised 'an experiment in the lighting of carriages at an expense not exceeding £100' in June 1888. This was devised by Thomas P Carswell, an assistant engineer at Cowlairs, and the son of chief engineer James Carswell. A conductor rail was placed inside the tunnel track where a pulley device under the carriages could make contact with it. Incandescent electricity then lit compartments with Swan bulbs in cylindrical glass fixtures on the ceilings. Two trains were soon fitted up, the power coming from a Crompton dynamo. Carswell was given charge of Queen Street's electric lighting and his salary was increased from £300 to £360 a year. The system was only given up in 1901 by which time

batteries below carriages could be charged by their rotating the wheels.

For the lighting of the regular NBR carriages, there was another scheme – Pintsch's Patent Oil Gas. This was prepared at depots and stored in tanks fitted below the vehicles. It gave a brilliant light, but there was a risk of fire and explosion. Even so, the NBR had 26 carriages adapted in 1886 for its use, and there was a proposal to light the Helensburgh trains by this means. However, it was not used on the GC&DR.

With short dwell times on the underground railway, the ease with which doors could be opened was an issue. Passengers were accustomed to leather straps in compartments that had to be pulled to lower the window, then a hand had to be extended to grasp the outside handle. There were protests about this inconvenient system and so handles on the inside were installed. But then there was a further problem – children interfered with these,

Finnieston station had a restricted site lying in a deep cutting west of Charing Cross and was the scene of a collision on account of the 'thick atmosphere' in 1886. (RailScot)

The lighting of carriages perplexed passengers and the NBR experimented with electricity in the tunnels on the G&CDR. (Mr Punch's Railway Book/Gutenberg)

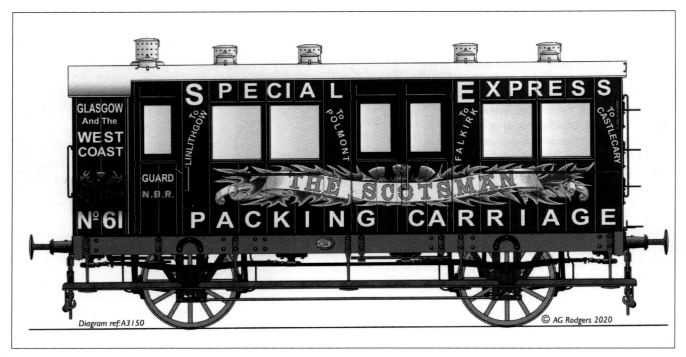

Conveying newspapers was big business for railway companies and the NBR had special arrangements with vans for 'The Scotsman'. (Allan G Rodgers)

and so 'Wethered's Patent' handles, that claimed to be 'tamper proof', had to be purchased.

Keeping people informed about railway activities, appointments and performance were now regular features in newspapers. These displayed advertisements for excursions, special offers and service information; they also carried reports of shareholder meetings and highlighted new locomotives and carriages. The press also described accidents, consequent legal proceedings and any compensation claims that arose – not always favourably for the NBR.

The railways played a key role in the growth of the newspaper industry. As early as the 1830s newspapers were being carried on trains as 'parcels', a faster system than 'goods'. By the 1880s millions of papers were being produced and read in Britain each day. Queen Street station became one of Glasgow's key centres for handling this traffic. On the NBR, the 'North British Daily Mail' and 'Weekly Mail' were being carried at £325 a year for three years. By 1887, the proprietors of 'The Glasgow Herald' had made a five year agreement for £1,000 a year – less any share paid by other newspapers – for a special train from Glasgow to Edinburgh, and £550 a year for any newspaper conveyance by ordinary trains. Soon there were contracts covering a range of publications such as the 'Scottish People' and the 'Scottish Athletic Journal'. There were also distribution arrangements – Glasgow papers going only to places 'south of the Tay', while Edinburgh evening papers were not to be brought to the west.

Such business was a nightly activity with newspapers 'hot off the presses' being rushed in parcels on horse-drawn vehicles to railway sidings where loading into vans took place. The

railways also carried the rolls of newsprint and gallons of ink to the newspaper offices that sustained the trade. In addition to daily papers, Glasgow soon had three evening papers, often in several editions – these were the 'Evening Times', 'Evening News', and 'Evening Citizen' – titles shouted by vendors as passengers hurried to Queen Street and other city stations on their way home. The importance of newspapers in improving literacy and educational standards by spreading information and knowledge nationwide is often underestimated, as is the solid contribution that the railways made to this whole process.

With over 200 trains passing through the tunnels daily, the Low Level station at Queen Street became notorious for its perpetual 'smog' of steam and sooty smoke, but at least there were large openings to serve as smoke vents at either end of the tunnels. Much worse was Charing Cross which was set in what was then an 'up market' residential part of the city's West End. The station was also close to the fashionable shopping venue of Sauchiehall Street and to the King's Theatre. Here the railway rose at 1 in 200 in both directions towards Charing Cross station that was contained in a long tunnel.

Air pollution was now receiving greater attention and James Marwick, the Town Clerk of Glasgow and an experienced adversary of the NBR, was soon taking action. In the course of the 19th century, there was a movement towards smoke abatement in Britain – 'The Railway Regulation Act of 1868' made ' provision for the improved control of pollution ...prejudicial to health or a nuisance'. In Scotland, public and private 'nuisances' were the same – circumstances where public health was affected,

personal discomfort was experienced, or material damage was caused to property.

In October 1887, a letter from Glasgow's City Architect had complained about the conditions at Charing Cross station, and in December a report by the NBR engineer was submitted to the board. No action resulted. The following August, the NBR general manager had received another letter from the Town Council about the enlargement of the station as a possible 'cure'. In December 1888, note was taken of a plan

Top: The Glasgow International Exhibition in 1881, and subsequent similar events, brought increased passenger traffic to the railways. (Glasgow University Library)

Left: The exhibition, promoting 'industry, science and art', also advertised excursions by rail and steamer. (Glasgow University Library)

Far left: Glasgow's exhibitions became renowned with railway companies running 'cheap excursions' on trains that by the 1900s had enhanced passenger facilities. (Edinphoto)

prepared by Simpson & Wilson, the G&CDR engineers for the ventilation of the line and the matter was 'remitted with powers to proceed to the General Manager and two directors'. This scheme involved making four ventilating shafts opening into the centre of West Regent Street – at its intersection with the key city thoroughfares

John Conacher, appointed general manager of the NBR in 1891, found the company frustrating and old fashioned. (Railway Magazine)

of Main Street, Douglas Street, Pitt Street and Holland Street. The Corporation declined this scheme, citing interference and obstruction with city traffic and a direct violation of the GC&DR Act of 1882. The Magistrates were appalled at the threat of such destruction in the city centre.

A welcome diversion from the problems on the underground railway came in the summer of 1888 when the Glasgow International Exhibition of Science, Art and Industry was held in Kelvingrove Park from May to November. Opened by the Prince of Wales, it drew attention to the city and region's many achievements and aimed to raise funds for a museum, art gallery and school of art for the city. Perhaps surprisingly, Queen Street station did not appear in the arrangements as the royal party travelled by the West Coast to Motherwell and from there to the Caledonian Railway's Central Station the following day.

Railways were quick to take up the commercial opportunity presented by the exhibition, advertising ' The Best Holiday Programme: A trip to Bonnie Scotland – A Visit to Glasgow's Great World's Fair – The Only International Exhibition in the United Kingdom in 1888'. In January a joint railway superintendents' meeting was held at Perth about excursion and general railway arrangements for the exhibition. It proposed that all excursions be run to and from Queen Street High Level with appropriate tickets available, a scheme approved by the NBR. Hugh Paton, the railway's printer, supplied a 'Railway Diagram Poster of the NB lines in Glasgow' to assist excursionists. Notwithstanding the enthusiasm for the event, the railway companies refused to make free tickets available to the executives and organising committee.

With over 5.7 million visitors, the exhibition was an outstanding success. It had something

for everyone – its two main themes being industry and recreation. Over 60 per cent of the exhibitors were Scottish firms with Glasgow businesses to the fore. The recreational side had popular attractions such as a 'switchback railway' and trips on the River Kelvin by electric or steam launches. The press gave it the highest rating of any such venture held in over twenty years. Queen Victoria paid two visits when en route to Balmoral, but came from Renfrewshire to the St Enoch station of the Glasgow & South Western Railway. The Queen also opened the city's new Municipal Buildings on George Square when James Marwick was knighted for his long and distinguished service as Town Clerk.

Meanwhile, the ventilation issues on the underground railway continued. By January 1889, the Clerk to the Police Commissioners in Glasgow was writing to the NBR – complaints were continuing to be received from the public about the excessive smoke. Meantime, there had been a report from Major Marindin of the Board of Trade for providing 'most effectually the necessary ventilation' through the making of a large shaft in West Regent Street. This was at St David's Church, but the NBR board had no powers of compulsory purchase. The Major found the east end platforms at Charing Cross station 'hazardous' owing to the volume of steam and smoke making boarding a carriage dangerous; this 'existing nuisance' needed both the tunnel and the station to be opened out for proper ventilation.

At Town Council meetings, members described Charing Cross station as 'a disgrace to the age …in dense black smoke …with the people who patronise it running the risk either of being asphyxiated or being run over'. Conditions were 'abominable', had lasted for four years and the dilatory attitude of the NBR was inexcusable.

In 1891 a new general manager of the NBR was appointed. This was John Conacher who had begun his railway career with the Scottish Central Railway in 1861 before joining the Caledonian Railway, the company that took over the SCR in 1865. That year he went to the Cambrian Railway rising rapidly from accountant to secretary, and by 1885 to general manager. He was held in high regard in railway circles, moving to the NBR at a salary of £2,500, the same as that of the company secretary. Conacher brought a new impetus to resolving the dispute.

Individual members of Glasgow Corporation were now intervening on behalf of the citizens; in February 1892, Bailie Bilsland described Charing Cross station as 'disgraceful and dangerous' in a letter to the NBR – and he was ignored. By September, he arranged a Magistrates' inspection, all being members of the Police Commissioners' Committee. They traversed the covered portion – 310ft (94.4m) – in semi-darkness enveloped in steam and smoke as a train dashed past. Passengers could not see the platform edges and one had to be rescued by a porter after stumbling onto the track; several were willing to give evidence at a trial about the nuisance and danger at Charing Cross. The signals were not visible at 20yds (7m) on account of the thick atmosphere.

Soon it was reported that NBR proposals had been brought forward – more property on the north side of Elmbank Crescent would be purchased leaving Charing Cross station entirely open between North Street and Elmbank Street. To make it safer, the platforms would be widened, and on the south side of Elmbank Crescent, properties would be purchased to allay objections.

With the NBR's procrastinating, an action in the Court of Session was forecast. The Clerk of the Police Board intimated that unless within 14 days the NBR made satisfactory provision for the ventilation of the tunnel at Charing Cross in terms of the Act of Parliament 'an action of declarator and interdict without further notice would be served on the company' and its trains could be prevented from running.

This threat of legal action resulted in John Conacher, as NBR general manager, calling on the Clerk of the Police Board to say that the directors had another scheme under consideration, but he declined to give further details. The 14 day time limit expired, and after years of delay, on 4 February 1893 the Outer House of the Court of Session heard Counsel for the Magistrates of Glasgow as pursuers against the North British Railway as defenders. In court, it was stated that the railway company was bound by law to make all necessary provisions for the ventilation of the railway tunnel between Charing Cross and Queen Street. The action was taken under the Glasgow Police Act to which the attention of the NBR had been repeatedly drawn. For their part, the railway company argued that they had submitted a scheme in December 1888 with ventilating shafts close to West Regent Street that had been declined. After further delay, the NBR then proposed ventilating the railway by means of a shaft on a feu on the east side of Blythswood Square – for which a warrant giving permission had been granted by the Corporation in July 1891. Nevertheless, no action was taken despite numerous requests from the Corporation for the NBR to proceed.

Once in the Court of Session, a 'last minute' announcement stated that the NBR would make alterations to the tunnel and station that would meet the Corporation's requirements. However, Parliamentary powers would first have to be obtained. The action was then 'sisted' or paused,

giving a chance for the parties to negotiate with a view to a consensus. Eventually, early in 1894, the Marquis of Tweeddale as chairman of the NBR, signed an agreement with the Corporation of Glasgow about improvements at Charing Cross station. A contract followed in March for which Simpson & Young were the engineers.

Unless NBR shareholders had followed reports of Town Council business in the newspapers, only in February 1893 were they told about the serious ventilation problem between Queen Street and Charing Cross stations and about the longstanding dispute with Glasgow Corporation. The NBR had finally agreed to the opening out of the 'covered over' portion at Charing Cross making the station 'better adapted to the large traffic which is now conducted there'. Obtaining Parliamentary authority cost £40,000, but acquiring land and carrying out additional works was £200,000.

It was 1895 before the works of improvement at Charing Cross station were completed. The east end had been 'unroofed' and the total length was now 530ft (161.5m) of which half was glazed with ample space at both ends for the escape of smoke and steam. The platforms were now wide with waiting rooms on each, while the signal cabin had been moved to the north platform and there were hoists for luggage.

Just as with the ventilation problem on the GC&DR, the NBR was slow to respond to making its railway safer. The outcome was a draft order from the Board of Trade in 1889 requiring the

Charing Cross station after the tunnel had been opened out by 1895 and improved station facilities built. (R W Lynn)

Workmen's trains on the NBR usually consisted of old four-wheeled carriages with most compartments 'non smoking' as men chewed tobacco. (Allan G Rodgers)

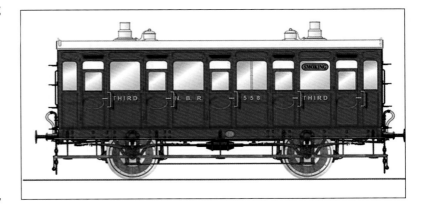

Locomotives with their trains were hauled up the 1 in 41 Cowlairs Incline until 1908. Here a Drummond 4-4-0 tank engine NBR No. 90 copes with a local service in 1898. (Dr Tice F Buddon)

company to proceed with 'the Block Telegraph, with Interlocking Points and Signals', plus the installation of continuous brakes on its vehicles. Only now was the response from the board immediate and 'best efforts' would be made to comply with the order.

With the NBR board having held out against any move towards workers' rights and trade unions, the company was now confronted by the Secretary of the Amalgamated Society of Railway Servants campaigning over 'hours of duty' for staff and payments for overtime. By November 1890 a circular prepared by the society was approved. When senior goods clerks requested an increase in salaries, the general manager would only allow 'a slight increase in the most deserving cases'. For staff, a committee would consider a superannuation fund and contributions could now be made to the NBR Insurance Company, set up in 1855, that arranged small pensions, awards for injuries and donations to hospitals.

The Low Level station had its share of mishaps, and on 10 July 1893 when a 17 coach workman's train derailed, the driver and fireman had been on duty for more than 12 hours. Notwithstanding, a delegation of employees was unable to get the NBR board to alter hours of work 'unless the Caledonian do the same'. An

observer was unimpressed by the NBR, noting that it was 'unpunctual and had undermanned stations where duties were done in a listless manner' – so much for employee loyalty.

The 'E&G' main line linking Glasgow and Edinburgh was of the first importance and the busiest. The ambition was to run a train every hour with the expresses taking one hour for the journey – which the top locomotives should be able to accomplish. What Conacher found was discouraging – an antiquated system with a wire rope-worked incline at a city terminus. Trains were still assisted out of Queen Street by the winding engine at Cowlairs, while incoming trains had their locomotives detached there and were brought down the incline in the care of brakemen on brake wagons as they had been since 1842. There was now congestion of traffic at Cowlairs waiting descent with consequent shortages of stock at Queen Street and delays to services.

So Conacher held trials with locomotive-hauled trains that were successful, and he therefore advised the NBR board to give up rope haulage. Nevertheless, he was of the opinion that much more should be done – his recommendation was to quadruple the line from Cowlairs to Bishopbriggs. This would mean driving a second tunnel between Queen Street and Cowlairs.

The NBR directors considered the proposal for six years and with traffic growing, there was increasing chaos that seemed insoluble. Only in September 1898, did the directors take the decision to seek Parliamentary powers. In the event, the line was never quadrupled and rope assistance out of Queen Street continued for another decade. Were the directors in fear of a descending train running out of control, or by the level of investment that would have to be faced in driving a parallel tunnel? A second portal, now hidden behind the inevitable 'grey boxes' is a reminder of Conacher's intention. After boardroom infighting, this far-seeing manager left the NBR the following year

The signal box at Queen Street was on a gantry with the tunnel mouths beyond; the right hand portal had a short head shunt for the goods yard. (Railway Magazine)

.**Chapter 5**

A New Century with New Challenges

In 1899 James Calder, the NBR's assistant general manager, gave an account of Queen Street station – noting that it was remarkable as 'no engine ever brings a train into it' – instead these relied on 'two stalwart brakesmen in heavy wagons' for a safe descent from Cowlairs.

The High Level station now had six platforms, varying in length from 280ft (85m) to 680ft (207m) and in width from 18 to 33ft (5.4 to 10m), with the goods yard bringing the total area to 7 acres, or 28,000m². There were ten lines of track controlled by 45 signals on a gantry close to the tunnel mouth. An electric bell from platforms was rung when a train was ready to leave. The High Level handled 115 trains most weekdays, but this 'was attended with the greatest difficulty' on account of the rope-assisted incline. Only 7 minute intervals were allowed for the departure of trains going up the incline – mostly nine per hour being sent off. Any shunting had to be performed in the tunnel. The station's main distinction was its 'gracefully designed ... segmental glass roof'.

At the High Level, the day began with a loco workman's train at 5.30 for Cowlairs workshops. Through the night, a newspaper express for Edinburgh left taking the Glasgow papers in parcels for Scotland's north, south and east. By 5am a similar train came from Edinburgh with 'The Scotsman'. The last train of the day was at 11.20pm.

Prime activities were the trains to and from Edinburgh – an average of 33 per day, but only three on Sundays, the expresses taking one hour and 10 minutes, and the slow – stopping trains at wayside stations – 15 minutes longer. The station clock at Queen Street would be keenly watched as the NBR was not noted for punctuality and the rope-assisted incline did not help smart working – unlike the rival Caledonian Railway that advertised its services as 'True to Time'.

The opening of the Forth Bridge in March 1890 had brought new travel possibilities at Queen Street. Access from Glasgow via Winchburgh Junction to the Fife Coast with its 'bracing watering places' and to St Andrews for 'the golf' was now possible. Aberdeen was also accessible as the North British had running powers over Caledonian tracks from Kinnaber Junction north of Montrose. The 'Aberdonians' via Dundee had a best journey time of 4 hours 10 minutes, though the Caley from its Buchanan Street station, and running by Perth and Forfar, took 15 minutes less. Special note was also taken of the 'Fort Williams' with their fine corridor carriages. These used the Glasgow, Dumbarton & Helensburgh Railway via Maryhill and Westerton, thus linking Queen Street High Level both with the tourist route and with growing suburbs.

There were also services to London King's Cross by 'the North British and Great Northern' – the NBR did not mention the North Eastern Railway, a company with which it had a fraught relationship. By 1900, there were through carriages on two daytime and three overnight

From George Square, the North Street entrance to Queen Street station shows the North British Station Hotel (right) before enlargement and an electric tram car c.1900. (Postcard & covers)

A map of the railways in and around Glasgow c 1900 shows the terminal stations in close proximity to the city centre. (Glasgow Stations - J R Hume & C Johnston)

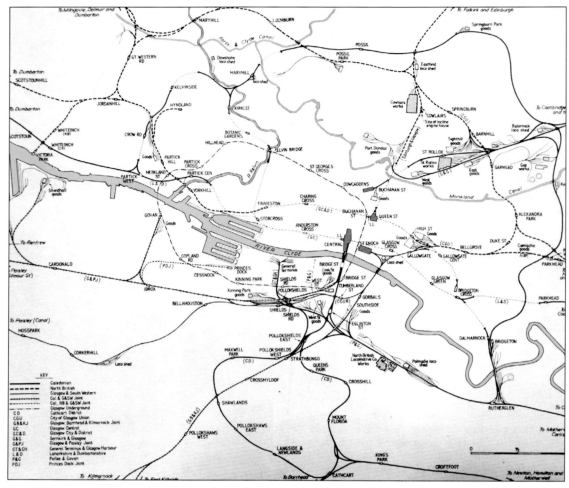

trains (two with a sleeping carriage) out and back on weekdays. Leaving Queen Street at 8.45am would bring passengers into London at 6.30pm – a journey of less than 10 hours.

The High Level had waiting rooms according to ticket class, a 'moderately sized refreshment room' and kiosks for 'fruit, tobacco and books'. There were facilities for left luggage, and a convenient cabstand alongside the main arrival platform. The booking office, enlarged by some extra 'windows', was adjacent to the Dundas Street courtyard. Between Queen Street and St Enoch stations, the 'Transit Department' ran a horse-drawn omnibus – free to ticket holders.

From a platform end at Queen Street c 1910 NBR tank engines and an abundance of advertisements are seen. (A E Glen)

According to railway regulations, there should have been an inquiry office to assist passengers, but the NBR got round this by having 'two train indicator boards' displayed at platform ends – these showed destinations, departure times and platform numbers.

To add to the complexity at the High Level station, the goods yard on the east side was busy with an average 31 'lifts' of wagons in 24 hours between Queen Street and Cowlairs. The parcels traffic was large, requiring 15 vans for deliveries in the city.

Running the show was the 'District Passenger Superintendent for the Western Division' whose office was in the Wardlaw Kirk. It also housed the chief goods manager, the outdoors manager, the plant superintendent, telegraph department and their staffs.

The Low Level station with its four lines was well used. Its long central island and side platforms (with lifts and hydraulic hoists for luggage) had a throughput of 430 trains on weekdays. The small signal boxes on bridges at the tunnel mouths directed 24 trains an hour at busy times.

The Low Level line's importance was growing as it connected the city's densely populated east end with the docks, shipyards and engineering works on its west side. Regular services were workman's trains to Kilbowie for the Singer

Left: *Craigendoran station was opened in 1892 to serve the NBR's steamer port. (Railway Magazine, 1899)*

Right: *The lavish interior of a NBR first class saloon for West Highland services. (Railway Magazine. (1899)*

factory and to Clydebank for J &G Thomson's yard (latterly John Brown's). There were also services east calling at Parkhead for Beardmore's Forge and other industrial sites. The four Low Level platforms had trains at five to six minute intervals, but some were making just three minute calls – a tall order when stopping and starting a steam locomotive on such services. The intensity of services often put the Low Level in a state of smog in spite of its having large openings at both tunnel mouths. Nevertheless, the Low Level had to be braved by Glaswegians travelling to Craigendoran for the steamers, an instruction stating that such passengers were 'not booked by the High Level Trains to and from this station'.

There had long been opposition from Helensburgh people to a steamer port, but in 1882 two jetties were built at Craigendoran, further east, on a spur from the railway. This enabled the NBR to make a serious attempt for a share of the growing commuter and tourist traffic on the Firth of Clyde. From just two steamers in 1870, the NBR fleet grew to seven by the 1900s, all having names from Sir Walter Scott's writings. There were many regular services to Helensburgh and other Clydeside stations; however, the 'crack' trains were the 'Boat Trains' from and to Craigendoran – especially the 8.52am and the 4.10pm for those commuting by steamer.

Watching football was a relief from the hard and dangerous work of factory and shipyard, or from the tedium of clerical or office duties. In the 1870s football based on Association Football rules soon came to prominence and early Scottish clubs began. By 1890 the Scottish Football League had been set up, and after professional status for players was accepted in 1893, club numbers grew rapidly. Local clubs soon had loyal 'home support', and the NBR carried throngs to matches, often from the Low Level station – Parkhead, going east from Bellgrove, was a station near the ground for Celtic Football Club. Queen Street also saw rugby enthusiasts travelling to games, especially to international matches in Edinburgh when

'specials' would be run from the High Level station.

To cope with crowds on match days and with overwhelming numbers at the Glasgow Fair, the inadequacy of access in and out of Queen Street station had to be addressed. In July 1892 a plan for improvement at the High Level had been submitted by the general manager, now George Wieland. This was 'the West Scheme' that focussed on Dundas Street. The company accepted that 'in house' engineering had to be supplemented by 'outside' expertise – and Blyth, Cunningham & Westland were appointed as civil engineers.

The peace of the realm was shattered between 1898 and 1902 by the South African War, described as a 'conflict of empire' – this saw much military movement on the railways. In 1892, the NBR had been asked to provide sixteen carriages for sick and injured soldiers. Earlier it had to ensure that cattle trucks were big enough to carry horses. Staff at Queen Street station would be familiar with both army 'regulars' – Glasgow had a barracks – and 'volunteers' on trains, the latter travelling at half fare when in uniform.

Although no longer 'Head Office', Queen Street had some two hundred employees. The Station Superintendent or Station Master had deputies, a quantum of clerks, and a range of other 'company servants', from passenger guards to porters and carriage cleaners, to supervise. The goods station had its own staff – with a manager and clerks, goods guards, porters, wagoners, carters and vanmen. A 'Western District Superintendent', with wide-ranging responsibilities, oversaw traffic inspectors and other senior staff. Cowlairs Works, where the Superintendent of the Line had his office, was the nerve centre for locomotive, carriage and wagon, signals and telegraph, and permanent way men. The latter had to ensure that track and signalling in and out of Queen Street station were kept in good order.

Regarding uniforms, the NBR had developed – as other railway companies did – a dress code

for its 'company servants' based on their status within the organisation. The Station Superintendent appeared on the platforms in a frock coat and tile hat. For others, the NBR specified the type of clothing and caps to be worn, and how frequently these would be replaced. The uniforms were dark blue, made from hundreds of yards of cloth supplied by a range of companies and manufactured into uniforms by J Smith & Company of Derby. The Store Keeper was left to 'arrange purchases on the best terms' and should be advised about any 'transfers, promotions or appointments'.

From the earliest days of the railways, hotels for passengers in transit were established by

railway companies – those at London Euston and Birmingham New Street being notable examples. Scottish companies were slow to react – though the E&GR found itself in possession of properties that were leased out to tenants and run as hotels. The Wellington Hotel was an example. The presence of the railway station encouraged more, and by the latter 1850s there were ten hotels in George Square where merchants' houses were rapidly converted for this trade. Tracing the rise and fall of such establishments is complex; hotels brought problems for the NBR as owners, regarding maintenance, and frequent requests for reductions in rent. However, by the 1890s the 'age of the great railway hotels' was dawning and the NBR had to respond. The 'Ritz effect' on hotel management, and of Escoffier on menus, was being felt around Europe.

As the NBR found Queen Street station such a restrictive site, in September 1890 notice to quit was given to the tenant at the North British Imperial Hotel on the corner site at North Queen Street. The premises were then adapted as a Parcel Office. In August 1891, the name 'North British Station Hotel' makes its first appearance – on a George Square property that was leased out.

The NBR had already embarked on a grandiose hotel scheme at Edinburgh Waverley, and Queen Street station would now have similar attention. In November 1898 the board announced that a start would be made with its new hotel in Glasgow – there was talk of moving the goods depot to a site at College station. The board had taken the decision to demolish the existing North British Station Hotel and 'erect a more commodious building' in its place. In May 1902, the postponement of a sale of 'furniture, plenishings and stock of wines' at the hotel was advertised, but 'owing to the King's Visit' and enquiries 'for rooms and windows', this had been deferred. A royal visit gave a business opportunity that was not to be missed. In the event, the Coronation and visit of King Edward VII were delayed until 1903 owing to his illness. Only then were the premises 'entirely gutted' and another storey added, while the interior was reconstructed on 'fire proof principles'.

In 1903 Queen Street station featured in a royal programme, its first in over fifty years – if the visit by the Shah of Persia in 1889 is discounted. A special NBR train brought King Edward VII and Queen Alexandra from Dalkeith over the E&G route to Glasgow on 'a dull day in May that did nothing to enhance the terminus'. The NBR had made efforts to improve its look with 'pines, palms and flowering plants'. The station was closed to the public but 'a few hundred railway servants' did have access, viewing the royal arrival from 'comfortable and advantageous lodgement on the roofs of several corridor carriages in a side lye'. The NBR's 'royal train' was brought down the Cowlairs incline into the station with brake wagons in the usual way, but on the royal party's return, they were not exposed to the slow ascent as they left Glasgow from Maryhill station.

An improvement for services at Queen Street station came in 1904 with the opening of the new engine shed at Eastfield, close to Cowlairs. With 14 roads, it was capable of accommodating 84 locomotives. That summer for the Glasgow Fair Holidays, the NBR had a 'Programme of Cheap Bookings' with 'Return Tickets at the Single Journey Fare' to over 60 stations on its routes. Extra steamer sailings with tours round Bute were popular, and to avoid overcrowding at booking offices, excursion tickets could be got until 10pm. For employees, payments for overtime were now accepted along with three days of paid holidays in the year.

The rebuilt North British Station Hotel opened in May 1905. It was 'practically new', with its main entrances fitted with revolving doors, an American 'fun' invention to prevent draughts. All public rooms were finished in mahogany – lounges, smoke room, writing rooms, bars, public restaurant and dining room. The kitchen had the latest appliances, the grills 'being open to the diners' view'. A wide staircase, plus an elevator, reached all floors where there were 105 bedrooms, 24 being 'en suite'. There were steam-heated radiators; electric lights shone from 'tasteful electroliers', while electric fans gave 'perfect ventilation'. Furnishing was on 'a sumptuous scale' and an alarm clock system was 'wired' to bedrooms to help guests catch early trains. The telegram address was 'Attractive, Glasgow', and the manager W T Willder was probably recruited from the Continent.

Some attention to passenger comfort was being given to NBR trains; from 1898, its 8-wheeled coaches had internal side corridors allowing access to lavatories. Nevertheless, a policy of 'make do and mend' resulted in old six-wheelers appearing on some express services. Then in 1905 the Caledonian introduced 12-wheeled carriages on its expresses from Glasgow and Edinburgh to Aberdeen – handsomely appointed, these were 'luxury travel at the ordinary fare', with vestibule connections allowing access to dining cars. The NBR had to respond and in 1906 brought out 'block trains of fixed formation', with nine vestibuled carriages with electric light and steam heating; a dining car was an innovation for the NBR.

Such developments greatly increased the weight of trains and more powerful locomotives were soon ordered. In 1906, the first 4-4-2 Atlantics were built for the company – impressive engines that carried names and

acquired a legendary status. In 1912 the first Scott class locomotives, fast and versatile 4-4-0s, appeared. However, the NBR had to keep an eye on costs – having an ever longer mileage through the opening of branches and the doubling of existing lines did not necessarily bring more revenue. This led to worries about the amount of 'unremunerative running' to which Queen Street station added a large share. This arose from movement of empty stock from carriage sidings to and from the station and the return of light engines to turn or to go 'on shed' two miles away at Eastfield. The total reached 20,300 miles in a four week period – almost half for the whole NBR network. Yet the proposal to install a turntable and water column at Queen Street to ease the situation was turned down as 'two roads' at its goods facility would have been lost.

Although trains of *empty* carriages were being successfully removed from Queen Street station up the Cowlairs incline by locomotives without the assistance of wire rope haulage, it was only in December 1907 that the decision was finally

By 1906 the NBR had 'block trains' of corridor carriages with vestibule connections, electric light, lavatories and steam heating. (J.Salmon postcard)

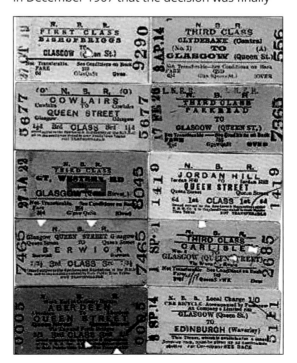

A selection of NBR tickets shows the diversity of places served from Queen Street station. (Michael Stewart)

Heavier trains required stronger locomotives – here a NBR 4-4-2 'The Lord Provost' is remembered in this evocative painting at Queen Street station. (Dugald Cameron OBE)

taken to abandon the rope. Strong banking engines would now supply the extra power to assist trains up the 1 in 41 gradient. From 31 October 1908, six robust 0-6-2 tank locomotives, fitted with slip couplings, took on the duty at the tail of Queen Street's trains. With their performance proving satisfactory, on 26 August 1909 the incline rope was abandoned. Soon the stationery engine at Cowlairs was scrapped and the engine house became an electrical switch room. However, bringing trains safely *down* the incline continued to be problematic, depending on good brakes and driving skills – buffer stop collisions at Queen Street station were frequent. In August 1911, the brakes on the 1.05pm express from Edinburgh due in Queen Street at 2.10pm failed to act – and the train dashed against the buffers with such force that the engine mounted the concourse and crashed into the Refreshment Rooms. There were no serious casualties. The engine got a nickname – that of an American lady temperance reformer.

In 1892 a link from the GC&DR had been made from College to Bridgeton Cross (to which the G&SWR tied a spur in 1893) and the NBR

soon found a use for the Bridgeton station area – the storage of stock plus carriage cleaning facilities. By 1911 it had installed 'a large stationary vacuum cleaning plant' made by the Scottish Vacuum Cleaner Co Ltd of Glasgow. This was powered by a 16hp motor, tubes carrying the 'vacuum effect' to 'renovators' with nozzles. These proved ideal for cleaning cushions and upholstery, operators taking 10 to 14 minutes per compartment – a first treatment producing 8 to 9 lbs of dust per carriage – all being carefully recorded. This revealed how filthy NBR passenger vehicles were and the vacuum's benefits for public health. A fastidious approach was also taken to spitting – there were fines for this, but it was difficult to control on workman's trains when chewing tobacco was so prevalent.

By now, there was an uncertain peace due to rivalries between the British and the German Empires, both on the high seas and in Africa. In 1912 a Railway Executive Committee, consisting of the general managers of the major companies, was formed by the government. This was to ensure the co-ordination of rail services in the event of war when the railways would be taken over with existing managements carrying out national policies. There was however calm before the storm and in May 1914, corridor train excursions from Glasgow Queen Street 'with Cheap Fares to all parts of the Continent' were being advertised. Corner seats – much sought after – could be reserved with tickets issued in advance at the 'East Coast Office' in West George Street.

The conflict with Germany and its allies

From October 1908, powerful 0-6-2 tank engines, constructed at Cowlairs, assisted trains up the steep gradient from Queen Street station Here NBR No.862 awaits a turn of duty. (J F McEwan)

began on 4 August 1914. Immediately, War Office priorities caused expresses to be cancelled while 'specials' and freight took precedence. Territorial battalions were called up and troop trains marshalled. The Highland Light Infantry was the 'City of Glasgow Regiment' with two regular battalions, but from the commencement of the war, many territorial battalions were raised. An embargo had to be placed on NBR employees enlisting – 19 per cent attempted to join up – otherwise the railway could not have been run. The horrors of war were revealed in October 1914 when a special train arrived at Queen Street carrying 120 wounded soldiers and thirty stretcher cases for transfer to Glasgow's Royal Infirmary. Refugees also came to Glasgow – 15,000 fleeing from occupied Belgium, needing homes and support; 'undesirable aliens' were deported.

As the NBR had the largest network in Scotland, it became the liaison between the Scottish railway companies and Scottish Command. It had earlier pioneered a control system with traffic district headquarters communicating by telephone and telegraph with signal boxes – for the west, the centre was at Coatbridge. To identify trains, by day or night, headcodes using lamps were introduced.

In July 1915 some ongoing reconstruction works at Queen Street were reviewed. The Parcels Office would transfer to a 2-storey brick building on the goods yard site, with access from North Hanover Street. Elevators would lift bags of parcels to and from station platforms. With the war effort, 'Parcels' was busier than ever, despatching army consignments and knitted 'comforts' for the troops. The intention was to transform the West George Street frontage with 'the refreshment rooms under the clock' being removed to open up a new main entrance. Management offices would go to the former Royal Hotel across North Hanover Street. The complete scheme was estimated to cost up to £40,000, but wartime conditions put a stop to it.

Although materials were soon scarce, additional locomotives and rolling stock had to be constructed to support a huge increase of 136 per cent in NBR goods and mineral haulage. As the priorities for passenger traffic were military, Glasgow-Kings Cross trains no longer ran and fares went up 50 per cent. Stations were closed to save manpower and other resources; soon 800 women and girls were employed as clerks, gatekeepers, ticket collectors and signallers. Pre-war, the only women employed by the NBR at Queen Street had been two 'office keepers', now there was a clerkess in the main office and another in goods.

The conflict continued for four years with devastating losses and campaigns waged far beyond Europe. The North British war memorial

carries 775 names to honour the memory of its railway men. When peace came in 1918, the railways were sorely depleted, with maintenance deferred and investment negligible. There were poignant scenes at Queen Street when 4,000 Belgian refugees, plus 300 tons of baggage, left for home that December.

Post-war, there were arguments in favour of retaining state control of the railways. William Whitelaw, the NBR chairman, protested against the low and unfair levels of compensation offered by the government when the NBR claim was £10million. The company was further disadvantaged in 1919 when Eastfield shed went on fire and 19 locomotives were destroyed. The NBR board was completely opposed to the amalgamations of the private railway companies promoted by the government. Nevertheless, in 1921 a Railways Act saw 37 private railway companies being merged from 1 January 1923, and the 'Big Four' established – the Great Western, the London & North Eastern (LNER), the London Midland & Scottish (LMS) and the Southern Railways.

For Scotland there were two companies – the LNER inheriting the East Coast routes, by taking over the North British and the Great North of

Typically on the tail of trains, the banking engines gave assistance until the 1960s, but they also took empty stock to carriage sidings at Cowlairs. (K. Jones)

The cap badge of the HLI, the Highland Light Infantry, the City of Glasgow regiment, in which many railwaymen tried to enlist.

Nigel Gresley of the Great Northern Railway became Chief Mechanical Engineer of the LNER in 1923. His designs, notably of the A4 class, became legendary. (Institution of Mechanical Engineers)

Scotland Railways, and the LMS by absorbing the Caledonian with its West Coast main line and network, plus the Glasgow & South Western and the Highland Railways. William Whitelaw became the first LNER chairman, a welcome appointment. The new company had a decentralised system with a general manager and local directors for Scotland. With Queen

THE QUEEN OF SCOTS
PULLMAN

leaves GLASGOW *(Queen Street) at* 10 5 am | *week-*
and EDINBURGH *(Waverley) at* 11 15 am | *days*

for KINGS CROSS, LONDON

Through connexion for the Continent via Victoria

The Queen of Scots Pullman' began running from Queen Street station in 1928 with trains on weekdays to London King's Cross. (Vintage Poster Shop)

Street station now a key LNER terminal, many changes took place – there were 'modern' uniforms for station staff, new liveries for locomotives and rolling stock, and different instructions to follow.

Some pre-war schedules from Queen Street returned in 1919 – the best E&G trains again taking 65 minutes to and from Edinburgh. Summer services to Crail by the 'Fife Coast Express', or to the East Lothian golf courses by the 'Lothian Coast Express' – taking just 1 hour 40 minutes to North Berwick – were advertised.

'Normality' did not return with the peace as social and economic upheaval marked the interwar years with consequences for Queen Street station and its staff. A railway strike in October 1919 – about maintaining wartime wage rates agreed with the NUR (*National Union of Railwaymen*) and ASLEF (*Associated Society of Locomotive Engineers and Footplatemen*) – was successful. These unions also won the acceptance of standard rates across the rail industry plus an 8-hour day for members.

By 1924, Nigel Gresley from the Great Northern Railway, had been appointed Chief Mechanical Engineer of the LNER, and he was alert to the motive power deficiencies of the NBR. Soon a Great Central design of 4-4-0 was adapted for Scottish use; these 24 'Improved Directors', class D11, were capable of hauling heavy passenger trains. Maintaining a NBR tradition, they were given names from Scott's novels. When new carriages came, they were varnished teak, and NBR vehicles were relegated to secondary duties. New locomotives would now be constructed at Darlington or Doncaster, or by outside builders – henceforth Cowlairs was confined to overhauls and repairs, its last new locomotive emerging in 1924.

In May 1926 a General Strike was called by the TUC to stop wage reductions in coal mining – thereupon transport and heavy industry came to a standstill in solidarity with the miners. Volunteers tried to keep essential services running, but Queen Street saw very few trains. The strike fizzled out after nine days – but the miners stayed out causing lasting bitterness in union circles.

The LNER was Britain's leading coal railway carrying over 100 million tons a year from the rich coalfields that it served, but in 1929 came the Wall Street financial collapse. England's North-East and Yorkshire were hard hit by the ensuing trade depression and the LNER came close to bankruptcy. Even so, its board was intent on maintaining East Coast services and passenger numbers to counter LMS West Coast competition. Fast locomotives and prestigious trains with new levels of comfort caught public imagination. In May 1928, 'The Queen of Scots Pullman' with its 8-car all steel carriages had

begun running from Kings Cross via Leeds and Harrogate to Edinburgh and Glasgow, a luxury service at a supplementary fare.

At Queen Street, buffer stop collisions continued – in September 1928 *'when a London express was being shunted it ran into another train ... and five passengers received hospital treatment for shock'*. Worse followed in October when a train slipped back from the tunnel causing fatalities and many injuries.

By the mid-1930s, Queen Street's services had been speeding up with A1 and A3 Pacifics on the E&G route, while on suburban services

Gresley V1 and V3 tank engines were now regulars. The new 4-4-0 'Shires' were widely used on secondary routes from the High Level. Freight was in trouble – the recession caused a decline in goods and parcels traffic, and growing competition was faced from road haulage. Regulated rail freight pricing encouraged road hauliers to cut their prices, while bus companies attracted rail passengers with flexible routes, better frequencies and lower fares. Fighting back, the LNER advertised cheaper fares at 'off peak' times.

In response to MPs' criticisms about Queen

The LNER 4-4-0 No.2680 Lucy Ashton at Queen Street in May 1948 for a special excursion marking the 60th year of its namesake Clyde steamer. (A E Glen)

Gresley designed tank engines were active on the Low Level lines at Queen Street in 1957 when No. 67665 was seen on this Airdrie train. (Robin Nelson/NBRSG)

The station entrance at North Queen Street where the LNER displayed advertisements and motorcars were parked in the 1930s.

The concourse and platforms had retail opportunities:-

Left to right:-

Fruit, flowers and confectionary from Malcolm Campbell

Anderson's tobacco stall with slot machines adjacent.

*McLaren 'gentlemen's outfitters' window, beside a hoist to the Low Level.
(The engine is Shire No.2760 Westmorland).*

A stylish 'Art Nouveau' kiosk for Malcolm Campbell

The main bookstall of Robert Graham showing news of the arrival of RMS Queen Mary in New York in 1936.

(All Glasgow Life)

*No. 2 Booking Office dated from the 1855 improvements.
(D.Blades Collection)*

Top : *The busy concourse with train information boards and advertisements c.1930. (Glasgow Life)*

Below: *No.1 Booking Office had 'streamlined' structures to assist crowd movements. (D.Blades Collection)*

Street's inadequacies, plans to reconstruct the station and its hotel were announced in August 1934. It would be 'the biggest scheme of its kind undertaken by the LNER in the city since the war'. The station entrance would be rebuilt and hotel alterations would improve its dated lounge, dining room and bathroom accommodation. Only the hotel was given some attention.

Despite economic uncertainties and high unemployment, the Glasgow Fair continued to bring crowds to Queen Street. The warm sunny summers of the 1930s made going 'Doon the Watter' on the steamers attractive, and the LNER had some new vessels – 'P S Talisman' being diesel-electric. Nearer home, Hamilton Races drew crowds and Carntyne stadium, reached from the Low Level, was popular with dog racing

and 'dirt track' enthusiasts.

The storm clouds were again gathering over Europe with the rise of the German Reich and its aggressions. In 1938, loudspeakers were introduced at Queen Street 'for directing passengers and making announcements as the occasion arises'. Such occasions certainly came with the outbreak of the Second World War on 3 September 1939 when government control of the railways was resumed with a new Executive Committee managing the companies. Immediately all signage at stations that might assist an invading army was removed and military specials had priority. The evacuation of children from cities that were likely aerial targets had been tried out, but it was 'for real' in September when the Scottish lines carried 178,543 evacuees, with some parents and

The LNER paddle steamer Jeannie Deans was built for Clyde services in 1931 and is seen off Innellan that year. (A E Glen)

teachers, to safe locations in the countryside.

The LNER's Chief General Manager sent out 'Special Instructions for the Working of Railways' to be 'brought into force forthwith and observed by everybody concerned'. These covered the continuation of work during air raids, both of passenger and freight trains, and of breakdown, repair or maintenance gangs out on the line.

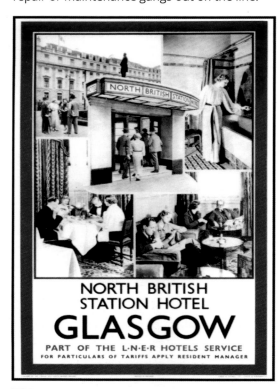

NORTH BRITISH
STATION HOTEL
GLASGOW
PART OF THE L·N·E·R HOTELS SERVICE
FOR PARTICULARS OF TARIFFS APPLY RESIDENT MANAGER

An advertisement for the North British Station Hotel, now in LNER ownership, after the interior was re-modelled in the 1930s. (Railway Posters)

Government messages had a colour code, the 'lights out' warning being 'purple'. All other staff should continue to work 'until danger is imminent in the immediate vicinity' – then resume work as soon as the danger was past.

'Damage or Fires, Unexploded Bombs or Parachute Mines' were listed as were the 'Movement of Trains in Gassed Areas'. Signalmen must keep their boxes locked and the windows were painted over leaving only slits of clear glass.

For station staff 'Air Raid Precautions' or ARP was stepped up with wardens on patrol and station lights obscured. Pre-war there were 15,000 engaged in ARP training in Glasgow but by early 1940 the number was 30,000. As Glasgow Central had a vast glazed roof, this was painted black, and it is possible that Queen Street glass got the same treatment – though smoke from below and soot from the city's chimneys were useful 'black out'. All staff carried gas masks and managements had to ensure that they knew – whether in offices or on platforms – the evacuation procedures for the station. At Queen Street, only public air raid shelters were to be used – the Low Level station and its tunnels were out of bounds for this purpose, and the station had to be cleared if the sirens went. Some employees were trained in fire fighting, some in gas decontamination, and others in first aid. Gummed paper strips appeared on office windows as a protection against shattered glass from bomb blast.

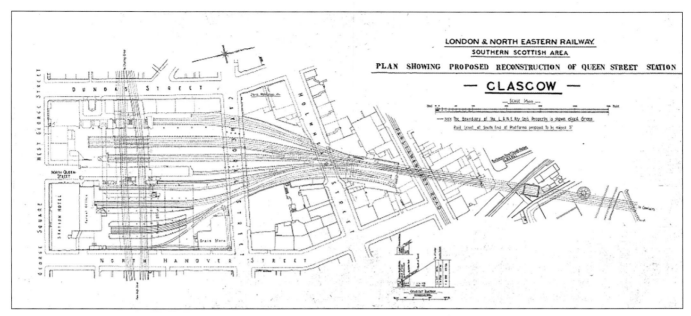

There were warnings about 'careless talk', and the movements of 'VIPs' were secret, such as 'Mr Churchill's visit' in January 1941. His special train with a saloon and restaurant car came from Waverley to Queen Street. He met Harry Hopkins, the Special Envoy sent by US President Franklin D Roosevelt, in the North British Station Hotel where Lease-Lend financial support for Britain in fighting Nazi Germany, was discussed.. Royal visits were not disclosed until after they had taken place. With the whole nation 'mobilised' for the war effort, labour became scarce, and by December 1942, advertisements called for youths as engine cleaners, willing to train as locomotive firemen, to sign up at Queen Street or at Waverley stations.

For ARP precautions, enginemen were instructed to limit the glare from locomotive fire doors, as stations, depots, key junctions and goods yards were vulnerable to aerial attack. As most industry was 'rail dependent', damage to the network was always a threat, and there were 'hit and run' attacks on targets in Glasgow. The worst destruction was the Clydebank blitz of March 1941 when much of the town and its infrastructure was destroyed. Thankfully, Glasgow's railway termini escaped unscathed.

Few non-essential trains ran and advertisements asked 'Is Your Journey Really Necessary?' Trains were very congested with compartments for six making room for eight or more passengers. Service personnel with kitbags packed the corridors, while platforms had canteens and food trolleys for troops in transit. As time passed, civilians were encouraged to travel by train to the countryside to help farmers producing food for the nation; most foods were rationed to provide 'fair shares' for all. Those 'lending a hand on the land' had to have 'emergency ration cards' for use in country

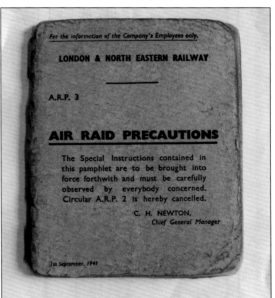

The proposed reconstruction of Queen Street station by the LNER in 1930 shows the short 'head shunt' tunnel from the goods yard. (Ask the Archivist, Network Rail)

An Air Raid Precautions booklet was issued to all LNER employees. (National Records of Scotland)

By the 1930s, Queen Street station comprised a range of properties – this former hotel was the Parcels Office. The policeman is on 'points duty'. (Glasgow Life)

After 1945, the railways were much depleted and nationalisation followed. Here a former LMS Class 5 in BR livery prepares to leave the station in 1960. (P Fisher)

After the war years, people rediscovered holidays and travel – at the Glasgow Fair in 1955, crowds queued for access to Queen Street station. (Glasgow Life)

shops. There was close supervision of retail outlets in stations – in 1943 the LNER was fined in Glasgow Sheriff Court for 'charging a halfpenny too much for a box of matches at their tobacco kiosk at Queen Street station'.

With cars laid up and petrol rationed, passenger numbers rose well above pre-war levels. Queen Street station also experienced the effect of military activities with big increases in its traffic flows. Glasgow was a key training centre for troops, with the Firth of Clyde an assembly harbour for convoys and a reception point for incoming American forces. Before D-Day, the allied invasion of Europe on 6 June 1944, there was immense pressure on the railways to move troops and freight trains conveying equipment and munitions south for the assault.

By VE-Day in May 1945, the railways in Britain were severely rundown. Intense usage hid their true condition – old locomotives and rolling stock had been kept running throughout the emergency. The Scottish network was largely intact but well worn by years of neglect. The post-war Labour government favoured 'nationalisation', the state ownership of the private railway companies and other key

industries. For railways, this took effect on 1 January 1948 when a Scottish Region of British Railways brought Scotland's railways under a unified management. Road and rail transport were co-ordinated through a British Transport Commission.

After the Second World War, the Bruce Report of 1945 proposed radical reconstruction for Glasgow's Inner City. Compiled by Robert Bruce, City Engineer and Master of Works, it would have done what Nazi bombing failed to do – totally destroyed the city centre including its four terminal stations, Buchanan Street, Central, St Enoch and Queen Street, plus such fine buildings as the City Chambers and the Glasgow School of Art. The city would then have got two new railway termini, described as 'modern and purpose built,' in an architectural style similar to that of the Empire Exhibition of 1938 – 'Glasgow North' being near the existing Buchanan Street station and 'Glasgow South' across the Clyde, replacing Central and St Enoch. The plan was never implemented on cost grounds.

Subsequently, shortages and inadequate investment did British Railways no favours. In 1951, with coal cheap and plentiful, the first steam-powered 'Standard' locomotive classes were completed. British Railways' choice of liveries then aimed to improve its look – it was Brunswick green for passenger engines (this hid dirt), lined black for goods, and crimson and cream for coaches (soon described as 'blood and custard). Train spotting, that had been tentative before the war, took off as a hobby. Queen Street was worth a visit to see its trains – typically with B1, Class 5 and occasional A1 or A3 engines at their heads. There might be echoes of the past with a Director or a Scott on occasion. Toiling on the tail would be a former NBR N15 tank banking the train up the incline to Cowlairs. It was just like the old days – but was that the problem?

Also in 1951 the Inglis Committee, appointed by BTC, reported on the desirability of electrifying the Glasgow and Clyde Valley rail network – provoking hostile reactions to the suggested abandonment of the city's extensive tramcar system. Inglis also favoured motorway and road improvements, both being desirable, and even suggested that Queen Street High Level could become a 'garage' – that is a multi-storey car park in the city centre. Its replacement would have shared a site at a new Buchanan Street station but the Low Level would have been retained.

In 1955 an ambitious British Railways Modernisation Plan was announced. This covered new trains, both electric and diesel, track work, signalling, some new station buildings and other infrastructure. It was now accepted that steam on the main lines would be

around until the 1970s. 'Modernisation' would be tackled region by region, but the Glasgow suburban electrification was given high priority. (Although electrification had been investigated by the Caledonian Railway for its Glasgow Central Railway in 1903, the only such investment in the city had been its early Subway, electrified in 1935).

In 1955 James Ness was appointed to head BR Scotland, and he pushed forward the proposal to electrify the Queen Street Low Level network. In August 1959, this closed to allow the reconstruction of stations, the raising of bridges and the installing of an overhead electrical system on 25kV. The new electric trains had open-plan well-lit saloons with sliding doors and exteriors with wrap-round windscreens styled by an industrial designer. On 7 November 1960, the 'Blue Trains' as the North Bank electrics were known, commenced public service, and they began a new era in passenger comfort, speed and cleanliness. It was intriguing to see the line ahead in a driver's view through the end windows. A double arrow sign, as their 'logo' was visible outside stations, on posters and on pamphlets. Queen Street Low Level was completely transformed into a bright and spacious station with two generous side platforms, well lit and tiled in pale blue. The central island was abandoned.

With patronage more than doubling, it was sad when explosions in transformers caused the withdrawal of the 'Blue Trains' from 19 December for 10 months. Steam locomotive haulage was restored – it was an immense achievement for Ness and his staff to resume such services, recalling staff to footplates, firing up engines and mustering coaching stock from sidings, with a provisional timetable soon available for passengers. When the 'Blue Trains' came back in October 1961, they again demonstrated comfort and quality possibilities for suburban travel, and the network soon spread through the city region and beyond.

In 1963 the Beeching Report, 'The Reshaping of British Railways' appeared. It was an attempt

by Dr Richard Beeching, a former ICI industrial chemist, and now chairman of the British Railways Board, to fulfil a government intention to make the railways pay by focussing on inter-city routes and long distance freight. One-third of the route miles in Britain carried just one per cent of the passengers, and over half the passenger stations (of which there were 4,300) had receipts of less than £10,000 a year. Consequently, his recommendation was that out of just under 18,000 miles (29,000km) of railway, 6,000 miles (9,700km) – mostly rural and industrial – should close. Described as 'rough and reckless', the report produced a barrage of criticism.

The railway had been contracting by some 150 to 300 miles (160 to 240km) a year, but this soared to over 1,000 miles (1609km) in 1964. Many stations served from Queen Street, such as Aberfoyle, Torrance and Kilsyth, had closed and Castlecary and Bonnybridge would follow. Bishopbriggs and Croy only escaped due to local campaigning and ministerial intervention. Terminal stations were also targeted with Glasgow losing both St Enoch and Buchanan Street. There was debate about the latter on its spacious site where a large modern terminus to replace awkward Queen Street could be envisaged. Nevertheless, Queen Street survived having two priceless advantages – its Low Level

Above right: The Low Level station had four tracks; here passengers wait on the island platform with mail about to be loaded on a Helensburgh train. (Roy Crombie/SRPS)

Above left: In 1959 work began on the electrification of the Low Level system; a steel bridge from P&W McLellan is being lowered into place by a steam crane on the rails below. (Glen collection)

Below: By 1956, Swindon diesel multiple units were on the E&G route – here alongside a former LNER A3 4-6-2 locomotive No.60042 Singapore at Queen Street. (Postcard & covers)

In November 1960, the 'Blue Trains' as the North Bank electrical multiple units (EMUs) were known, began running on the Low Level lines.
(J L Stevenson)

station with access to the suburban network, and a city centre location with proximity to Glasgow Central. In 1965 following a change of government, Barbara Castle as Transport Minister took a different view, and by 1968 the subsidisation of lines on social grounds was accepted.

From June 1956 'third class' travel had ceased when the term 'second class' was revived. A sign of BR's 'Modernisation' was soon on its way – dieselisation. For Queen Street passengers, this

move brought a succession of new travel experiences, initially on the E&G route – first with Swindon-built diesel multiple units with a choice of compartments, open saloons and buffet cars – all finished in shiny Formica. By the latter 1960s, intensive usage made their reliability questionable.

Accordingly in May 1971 diesel-electric Class 27 locomotives began 'topping and tailing' 6-coach trains of BR Mark 2 all steel coaches with modern interiors and enhanced safety

A key investment was the Travel Centre for passenger enquiries and ticketing with offices above for staff.

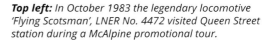

Top left: In October 1983 the legendary locomotive 'Flying Scotsman', LNER No. 4472 visited Queen Street station during a McAlpine promotional tour.

Topr right: Of all the BR diesels, the Class 37s became associated with Queen Street and Eastfield depot – this being No.37424 'Isle of Mull' in 1987. (RCTS)

Middle left: This BR Class 47 working a 'push-pull' service to and from Edinburgh is BR No. 47717 'Tayside Region' and is in ScotRail livery. (D Hinchcombe)

Bottom left: Class 170 DMUs, known as 'Turbostars', were regulars at Queen Street from the latter 1990s, this set being in Strathclyde Passenger Transport livery. (H.Llewelyn)

standards on the E&G. Journey times between Queen Street and Edinburgh on 'non-stops' were cut to 43 minutes – the best service ever. Sadly with intensive running and deficient maintenance, the locomotives also became fallible and punctuality fell. By 1974 track and signalling investment brought further upgrades when speeds of 100mph on the E&G were considered.

The transformation in the Low Level station only made the High Level station look neglected and old fashioned. There were soon attempts to 'modernise' it as the Commonwealth Games were coming to Edinburgh in 1970, and BR could benefit by increasing passenger traffic from Glasgow. The 'modernisation' scheme begun in 1967 had BR's own architects working with Bovis

Ltd as contractors on a project costing £200,000. It commenced with the removal of the Dundas Street arches and the old booking offices. No longer would passengers buy tickets at dark 'cubby holes' but in a well-lit Travel Centre of polished steel, glass and tiling, mosaics and murals, aimed at being 'modern and functional'. New ticketing systems were introduced giving a complete rail booking service. Staff offices were placed above the Travel Centre – the train shed's supporting Victorian cast iron columns being hidden in brickwork and white tiles.

BR also invested in re-designed track and platforms to allow the handling of the extra trains to Aberdeen and Inverness resulting from the 1966 closure of Buchanan Street station. Colour light signalling, controlled from a modern

The stone-cleaned Dundas Street arches and offices in the former church. Note the 'double arrow' sign advertising the electric trains. (J L Stevenson)

signal box at Cowlairs, was installed. Track circuitry now enabled half-minute movements of trains in and out of Queen Street – but the tunnel could only cope with one train each way at a time. A 'Telecommunications Centre for Scotland' was also constructed at Queen Street at a cost of £300,000.

Reconstruction at the former goods site on the east side now gave access to cars and taxis from North Hanover Street, but also entry to the parcels' office for 'Red Star' services – parcels business totalled no less than 424,879 items in

The classical church façade with preparations for demolition with the hotel extension in place (right). (Planning Department, Glasgow Corporation)

1968. There was also a loading bay for Royal Mail. New left luggage facilities were close to taxi ranks. For passengers, topping 3.2million a year, the concourse minus vehicle parking was much improved. The 'Roundhouse' cafeteria and bar had been modernised, and the dismal reputation of railway catering was at last being addressed.

The removal of the Wardlaw Chapel that had served as railway offices since 1855, and other properties fronting West George Street, had yet to come. It was all a question of money. Score Property Ltd, hoping for a pedestrian /retail development in Dundas Street, had taken an interest. By now 'air space' above railway properties was exciting developers. By 1975 there were plans for Consort House, a 6-storey office block on a 2-storey podium, designed by Miller & Black, a team that tackled a wide variety of projects. At street level, it housed the 'Hebridean' restaurant (given a Scandinavian look), and the 'Berlin' bar with a discotheque, both being supposed to 'catch the vibe'. On the station concourse, the 'Casey Jones' burger bar was a fast diner in line with similar high street trends.

From 1975 the North British Hotel – the term 'station' had gone – was part of British Transport Hotels (BTH), and it now had a 51bedroom extension, designed by BR's 'in house' architects. However, in 1983 BTH hotels were put up for sale, and though there was an effort to have a management buy-out, this was unsuccessful. The NB hotel, with its special place in Glaswegian affections, became first the 'Copthorne', and

The 150th year of the Edinburgh & Glasgow Railway in 1992 saw an A4 steam locomotive in Queen Street station carrying the name 'William Whitelaw', to honour a former NBR and LNER chairman.

then the Millennium, part of a global hotel and property chain.

Meantime, the Glasgow Subway had completed its modernisation in 1980, and its Buchanan Street station was linked to Queen Street station by a 'motavator' walkway and a curving canopy that sheltered passengers crossing Dundas Street.

After close on a century of use, by the 1970s the High Street tunnel was showing strain. There was a proposal to convert the 6.25kV section there to 25kV. (The former had been used on other portions of the electrified routes). In 1977-78 concrete slab track replaced ballast and timber sleepers, but soon silt from the hidden glacial valley below the line was seeping up and causing 'de-bonding' of the concrete sleepers. Innovative techniques were used to treat the problem and work began in 1982 using 'jet grouting' to stabilise the tunnel floor. This was followed by 'stitch and grout' methods as settlement was showing in the tunnel arch – enough overhead clearance had to be ensured for wiring. 'Mini piles' were used to underpin the tunnel walls and side beams inserted to give strength. All this was accomplished by short weekend possessions by March 1983 – notwithstanding the difficulties with a mass of utilities in George Street – at a cost of £400,000.

BR's Mark 3 rolling stock was now being deployed on the E&G – these all steel coaches of 'monocoque' construction with air suspension and disc brakes, were limited to speeds of 100mph on the line. Each set was worked by a Class 47/7 diesel locomotive with a remotely controlled driver van trailer (DVT) at the rear. This push-pull arrangement economised on

locomotives and the new coaches enhanced passenger comfort. On a regular interval timetable, it was publicised as 'The Shuttle'. With the DVT at the Queen Street end, the concourse was less polluted with exhaust and engine noise.

In 1981 after a long absence 'Inter-City' services between Glasgow and London Kings Cross were re-introduced at Queen Street with new high speed trains – HSTs – that were well received by passengers, and a touch of glamour came back.

1983 was when 'ScotRail' became the brand name for the Scottish Region of BR. A year earlier, Chris Green had come north as the BR operations manager and by 1984 he was general manager of the Scottish Region. Determined and innovative, for him, stations should be bright, clean and welcoming. This soon resulted in Queen Street's concourse being surfaced in cream terrazzo, with platform barriers for ticket

The driving trailer ends of coaches, adapted for push-pull operation with Class 47/7 locomotives at Queen Street in 1992 when on 'The Shuttle'. (Bruce Peter)

The new entrance at Dundas Street with its ScotRail canopy linking into the SPT Subway in 2016.

checks removed and red fibreglass seating installed.

There were further modifications at Queen Street Station when it closed for re-signalling in 1986. The following May, 'second class' became 'standard'. By 1990 the Sprinter DMUs were appearing – the Class 158s or 'Super Sprinters' for intercity services, such as the E&G trains, and the Class 156s for suburban and rural use in their ScotRail livery. Their main virtue was economy in operation and Queen Street soon echoed to their noisy motors.

Privatisation, proposed in 1991 to attract new investment, took effect in 1994. The highly integrated railway system was dismembered – it was back to the Canal Age with the infrastructure separated from whatever used it. On railways, the track, locomotives, rolling stock, and installations had all preferably been owned and controlled by the same company – and this made sense. A festive intervention came in 1992 when a steam locomotive was in Queen Street to mark the 150th anniversary of the Edinburgh & Glasgow Railway, and two former North British Railway locomotives were displayed in George Square.

Meanwhile, there was ongoing property

speculation around Queen Street station. The largest commercial property development and investment company in the UK was Land Securities Group PLC or 'Land Sec'. Begun by Harold Samuel in 1944, it moved from office development in London to retail warehouses and superstores in the provinces, and by the latter 1990s was involved in new construction projects. One of these was Buchanan Galleries, at the top of Glasgow's Buchanan Street 'spine' where the largest shopping mall in Scotland was constructed. It opened in 1998, bordered Queen Street station's west side and had a gangway in part above the railway's tunnel mouths that gave access to 2,000 car parking spaces.

The final dismembering of BR occurred in 1997 by which time many experienced managers had left to set up companies to profit by the new circumstances facing the railways. In 1999 the Class 170 Turbostars from Adtranz appeared and they played a key part in passenger travel from Queen Street until 2018. Though the 'ScotRail' brand was retained, a succession of 'TOCs', train operating companies, now bid for that franchise. From then on, Queen Street observers would see a variety of liveries or nametags on ScotRail DMUs – National Express, then First Group followed by Abellio. Meanwhile, the Low Level trains went from electric blue, through various oranges to carmine and cream. In 2004 a concourse-wide ticket gate was installed at the High Level to control access to platforms and protect revenue.

The Low Level station also had makeovers, including tiling in Strathclyde Transport's colours, and in 1986 was encased in bright yellow fibreglass that stopped troublesome drips of oil and water from tracks overhead. The new century with electrification proposals for the E&G would bring profound changes to Queen Street station.

The bright open concourse after the 'Chris Green' treatment in the mid-1980s. (D.Bowman)

Chapter 6

A Station fit for a Queen Street?

In 2007 the Scottish Government announced that the Edinburgh & Glasgow route and its associated lines would at last be electrified, a process to be taken forward by Transport Scotland and 'partnerships' formed between Network Rail, the ScotRail franchise and key contractors. This radical scheme became known as EGIP – the Edinburgh to Glasgow Improvement Programme. In 2012 the project was re-scoped by Transport Scotland. This resulted in a change from the proposed 6 six-car length trains per hour to be 4 eight-car length trains per hour. The Minister for Transport subsequently announced the redevelopment of Queen Street Station in July 2012.

The increase in train length led to a requirement to enlarge and redevelop the Station, there was concern about the possibility of an extension being made to the Buchanan Galleries Shopping Mall. This retail complex, the largest in Scotland, resulted from an investment by Land Securities Group PLC, a leading player in such speculations, and opened in 1998. In October 2014 Network Rail had proposed disposing of land and air rights at Queen Street station for the extension of the Buchanan Galleries Shopping Centre. Glasgow City Council was a party to the deal. This was to cost £390m and as a *quid pro quo,* the Buchanan Partnership, the Shopping Centre's owners, would provide 'new and enhanced station facilities'. For those who valued the station's daylight, ambience and open space at its platform ends, the thought of a Birmingham New Street development was 'dastardly'. There was also a question of ventilation as trains with diesel motors would continue to use the station. Both the Cathedral Street cutting at the tunnel mouth and the Dundas Street cutting at the west extremity of the Low Level station would have been lost. On 6 July 2015, shortly before work was due to start, the expansion with its 'air space grab' was 'paused' in other words, put on hold.

Land Securities still plan to undertake a development over the west Low Level cutting in the coming years. Planning for this was submitted to GCC in early 2020. Some preliminary activity on the east side of the station, where a large car park on the level had replaced a goods yard in the 1970s, was stopped, then cancelled – and this resulted in some further site clearance to remove steelwork. The site has now been used for temporary office accommodation for ScotRail

and for station construction teams. (There is also the possibility of a Platform 8 being placed there).

In the summer of 2016, as part of EGIP and Network Rail's track renewals programme, Queen Street station had become the focus of intense engineering activity resulting in the closure of the High Level for 20 weeks. Some trains were diverted to the Low Level and others to Glasgow Central. A diversionary route via Maryhill and Anniesland (where a new junction was made on a former rail site) also relieved some pressure. This enabled Edinburgh to Glasgow trains to access Queen Street Low Level from the west, then return to the capital via High Street. As part of Network Rail's renewals programme, the Cowlairs tunnel was given major attention, with its rock floor lowered by 1.5m prior to new replacement slab track system being laid and new drainage system installed.

As part of EGIP, the track layout at the tunnel throat was completely remodelled with seven new switch and crossing units. There was extensive platform demolition, followed by wall rebuilding, and a considerable part of the concourse at the buffer stops was excavated in preparation for platform lengthening and temporarily filled with polystyrene blocks. A new signal gantry spanning the north end of the station was built. Finally, in June 2016 the masts

Top: In 2016 with EGIP works at the station throat in progress, the bridging car park structure, spoiling the former open approach to the platforms, was apparent.

Below: It was bedrock and water at the north mouth of the Cowlairs tunnel when the floor was being lowered in June 2016.

Top: *A view up the Cowlairs tunnel from a platform end in June 2019 reveals its steep ascent.*

Below: *The Millennium Hotel extension and Consort House on West George Street.*

proposals showing a positive benefit to the Scottish economy and an enhancement of infrastructure would be welcome endorsements for obtaining such an order.

In 2014 there were two phases of consultation about the Queen Street station's redevelopment. These showed that there were reservations about a new structure being imposed on the heritage cityscape, and especially the effect it would have on the historic train shed. The works would take place in a Conservation Area where Listed Building Consent was required – the train shed being 'A listed' and the original portion of the Millennium Hotel 'B listed' by Historic Environment Scotland. Notwithstanding these considerations, the overall aim was to create a bigger and brighter terminus station and a better transport hub for Glasgow.

Only in September 2015 was the TAWS application finally submitted. As there were objections, notably from the owner of the Millennium Hotel faced with the loss of its 51 bedroom extension, the application then went before the Scottish Government's Planning and Environmental Appeals Division (DPEA). Its report came in October 2016 and stated that the removal of the hotel extension was necessary, and that the station works were in the public interest. Some adjustments were then made to the order, and conditions were laid down, including the formulation of a Code of Construction Practice. Only on 11 April 2017 was the TAWS order in its final form ready to take effect. The consultation documents had forecast an earlier resolution and start to the works.

The order was officially obtained by Network Rail during August 2018 when the possession of the crucial area on West George Street was secured. This was essential for making platform extensions, enlarging the concourse, improving accessibility and enhancing the station frontage. Network Rail announced that the project would be completed in March 2020.

From the outset, it was known that certain buildings would have to be removed – the 'in word' being 'deconstruct'. This applied to both Consort House, the concrete office block at the corner of West George Street and Dundas Street, and to the hotel extension, both dating from the mid-1970s and of mediocre quality. However, the project's environmental statement contended that both were of 'minimal architectural and historic interest'.

For supplying the works site and for the removal of spoil, a traffic management plan involving the M8 was developed; immediate access from West George Street to the station site was essential and a one-way system was put in place there. A taxi rank was relocated and arrangements agreed for the closure of the

were raised for the OLE wiring – efforts being made to minimise their intrusion in the historic train shed. By August, trains were running again and the passengers were back.

The first steps towards the re-modelling of the concourse and south façade of Queen Street station was for Network Rail, as owners, to acquire the powers to do this major work. Unlike past procedures, since 2007 an Act of Parliament has not generally been required in Scotland as a Transport and Works Order for a major project could be requested from Scottish Ministers. Any

street when required – such as those situations when large cranes were moved on and offsite.

As a preliminary stage for Queen Street station's redevelopment, Balfour Beatty PLC was awarded a £16million enabling works' contract. This was followed in August by the key £63million contract – the major investment that would see the demolition of the West George Street buildings and the construction of the new extension with its roof and façade. It would be a 'target cost' contract, whereby any gain or loss would be shared equally between Network Rail and the contractor; any 'overruns' above 10 per cent would have to be met entirely by the latter.

The task of producing a final design was given to Arup, with Building Design Partnership (BDP) architects led by Edward Dymock in the role of consultants. Their solution was a 'landmark' design, bold in style and innovative for a railway station. The façade facing George Square and West George Street would be fully glazed while the elevation to Dundas Street would have a series of interlinked volumes. The elements of the design would be tied together by a three-dimensional roof structure with a deep overhang and angled skylights above the concourse.

The design hinted at 'deconstructivist' trends in contemporary architecture, but the bold forms proved initially to be controversial. Some were dismayed that the style of the Victorian train shed had not been sufficiently respected and used as an inspiration for the reconstruction. Others bemoaned the chunky 'value engineering' that they believed spoke more of an engineer's view than of an architect's vision. The robust steelwork and other aspects of the design are in fact a protection against bomb blast.

In August 2017 an initial stage saw the removal of the ScotRail offices adjacent to Platform 1 and the relocation of the Travel Centre (or ticket office). This was displaced to converted premises on Dundas Street – in fact, to a former pub popular with off duty railway staff and enthusiasts, rumoured to be the only such facility in Glasgow where 'Real Time' train departures were beamed continuously. Several retail outlets on, or close to the existing concourse, were closed. The old entrance at North Queen Street was shut and traffic on West George Street became single lane beside the works site. Here lorries would bring supplies and hired equipment would have access. Hoardings were put up and decorated with designs by Gabriella Marcella, a graduate of Glasgow School of Art, who was inspired by the city Coat of Arms.

Above the former 'Travel Centre' on the west side of the concourse were ScotRail staff offices adjacent to Platform 2. The removal of these structures, with a view to extending Platform 1, went ahead when the station was closed at

Christmas 2017.

Some serious 'deconstruction' was now scheduled and Consort House was the target. The first stage was to 'encapsulate' the tower block in a scaffolding frame with external plastic sheeting. Always to be kept in mind was the location of the buildings close to the busy city centre of Glasgow, with both noise and dust having to be minimised. With the roof removed, in January 2018 two light weight excavating machines were lifted 36m up by crane to begin 'the top-down floor-by-floor' break up of the reinforced concrete structure and its steel frame.

Top: *Consort House was a 6-storey concrete block on a pilotus, with offices above and bar/restaurants below.*

Middle: *The temporary ScotRail Travel Centre in a former Glasgow pub in Dundas Street.*

Below: *The colourful 'wrapper' for the work sites was designed by Gabriella Marcella, a graduate of The Glasgow School of Art. (Network Rail)*

Preparations

Top: *Looking east, the work site on West George Street being prepared in September 2017.*
Middle left: *By October 2017 passengers had to 'hunker down' in the limited area at the platform ends.*
Middle right: *Ticket machines were set up on the margin of the narrow concourse.*
Above left: *The Travel Centre and staff offices on the station's west side would be removed.*
Above right: *A brighter commodious station was the plan - being realised by October 2019.*
Left: *The Balfour Beatty 'base camp' for work teams at North Hanover Street.*

Deconstruction

Top: *Demolition was well advanced on the Consort House site by June 2018.*
Middle left: *The first stage saw scaffolding up on Consort House by November 2017.*
Middle right: *Then came encapsulation to contain dust and prevent contamination.*
Above left: *Small excavators were craned up to 'deconstruct', floor by floor.*
Above right: *From George Square, the venerable train shed was being revealed in May 2018.*
Left: *Removing the hotel extension was by 'hand demolition' from October 2017.*

Vehicle Access

Top: *Road access had to be maintained at all times – here for insulation panels at West George Street.*
Middle left: *Transfers of equipment and materials between the work sites closed station access.*
Middle right: *Passengers to and from Dundas Street were temporarily stopped.*
Above left: *A Dem-Master lorry collects aggregate for recycling in January 2018*
Above left: *Concrete for foundations and screeding arrives at West George Street.*
Left: *A concrete tanker is a tight fit at Dundas Street in August 2018.*

J&D Pierce crane at the Dundas Street site in May 2019.

The 'paper deck' site above the Low Level lines under Dundas Street looking west towards Charing Cross.

The devices were remotely controlled. Thus the momentous site preparation phase began, conveniently using the lift shafts down which material was tipped. Steel reinforcements were extracted with special equipment – over 26,000 hours were worked during the process. Soon hand demolition, plus the use of long-reach excavators were removing the adjoining hotel extension.

Gradually, as seen from George Square, Queen Street's venerable train shed was revealed and ultimately a complete view was possible from West George Street. It gave a unique opportunity to see and appreciate the grace of the Victorian structure before it would be largely hidden by the new construction. Nevertheless, its exposure was not without risk from strong winds as the building from the outset had been sheltered by other structures. Temporary works were therefore done to give it more stability. Meanwhile, on the west gable of the hotel, an old sign for the former 'North British Station Hotel' was revealed.

Only in October 2018 was the 'deconstruction' finished when 14,000 tonnes of debris had been cleared from the site by some 1,000 lorry loads. To facilitate re-use of the rubble, a crushing plant enabled 94 per cent to be re-cycled and any steel was extracted prior to disposal. Lorry access was maintained off West George Street where in all 700 skips were filled, and removed from the station site. The recycling of the crushed concrete would see its reuse for aggregate in the construction industry – the aim was to recycle as much material as possible, thereby avoiding landfill and associated costs – with the added advantage of being environmentally friendly. Wood chippings were another by-product for use at equestrian centres.

In reviewing these tasks, Tom McPake, the Network Rail Programme Manager, emphasised the risks, "Demolishing redundant buildings in the heart of Glasgow and in a live station environment has been extremely challenging – over 47,000 passengers go through the station each weekday. Their safety was paramount'.

Only once the major structures on West George Street were removed, could the transformation of Queen Street station really begin. The programme of works was organised on a 'two front' methodology – the south flank lying between the existing train shed and West George Street, and the second facing Dundas Street.

The first project milestone on the Dundas Street side was reached on 7 May 2018 when the extension to Platform 1 became operational. This had been lengthened by 50m to take four-car trains, making good use of the space left by the removal of the offices on the station's west side.

The Network Rail staff and the Balfour Beatty teams were accommodated in George House, across North Hanover Street from the station. Close collaboration was therefore possible and has typified the project based on 'open and honest working arrangements'. Another advantage was the proximity of the many local sub-contractors who were within a 30mile radius of Glasgow. This allowed the project team to visit suppliers, thereby facilitating the monitoring of progress; examples of such locally based contractors being J&D Pierce, based at Glengarnock, who supplied the structural steelwork, and Curtis Moore at Hillington who carried out roofing and insulation. There was also a reduction in carbon footprints through the shorter distances travelled in making deliveries.

Project managers pointed out that there had been substantial benefit from the use of a 'single three-dimensional model' of the station works developed as a result of working with BIM level 2 software. Using 'virtual reality' headsets, this had given 'walk-through' impressions, and proved a very useful tool during consultations and visualisations. It reduced possible design and construction disagreements, or misinterpretations, notably when devising the project's later stages when various sub-contractors would be working in the same area, such as the basement.

Although the operation of the Low Level station was not directly affected by the works, access to its platforms had to continue, and both fire and evacuation procedures had to be maintained. There were also weight restrictions above the tunnels to consider. An old concrete structure, well covered with litter, and known as the 'paper deck' at the west mouth of the tunnel was removed in December 2017.

The installation of escalators between the station's two levels has not been attempted, the reasons being serious lack of space and probable cost, but there are lifts available.

The challenges of working in such constrained site conditions – with only one main access for vehicle movements at West George Street – were encountered daily. Effective co-

Top: *Preliminary works in progress at the 'paper deck' site at Dundas Street in February 2019.*
Middle left and right: *Steel supports to carry the new bridge being constructed in March 2019.*
Above left: *Beams for the new bridge are lifted over the rails in March 2019.*
Above right: *The steel frame for the new office structure goes on top in April 2019.*
Left: *A westbound train at Platform 9 in January 2020 with the new bridge above and the tunnel to Charing Cross ahead'.*

Groundworks

Top: *The train shed's south frontage was exposed by September 2018 when the basement excavation was progressing.*

Middle left: *Piling beside the former North British Station Hotel site.*

Middle right: *Shuttering goes up at the former chapel site in October 2018.*

Above left: *Works advance on the east side with a major drain structure in view.*

Above right: *The entrance at Dundas Street, seen in June 2019, is 'blast strengthened'.*

Left: *Concrete being poured at the west side in March 2019.*

Above: *By November 2018 at West George Street, concrete pouring and reinforcement was ongoing at the east side.*

Left: *After excavating as much as 8m down, the basement takes shape on the west side.*

West Flank - Dundas Street

Top: *This view south in Dundas Street in June 2019 shows the formidable steelwork for the offices and station entrance in place.*

Middle left: *By May 2019 framework for the new offices had reached roof height.*

Middle right: *Summer evening action - putting a steel beam into place in May 2019.*

Above left: *'Just a wee touch more' – adjusting an alignment that evening.*

Above right: *The robust construction of the passenger entrance from Dundas Street in June 2019.*

Left: *Preparing elements for the steel structures at the work site in Dundas Street.*

ordination within the station was ensured by having a full-time ScotRail representative funded by Network Rail in attendance as part of the project. Following the Code of Construction Practice, especially with respect to the Millennium Hotel, there was minimal disruption and liaison was good.

Once the office block and the hotel extension had gone, and with the 'deconstruction' complete, there was now an empty site lying alongside the train shed. Here observers could see evidence of the blond sandstone that the old quarry had once supplied. Excavation and piling soon opened up a 'basement', 4m below street level that would be a crucial part of the station's reconstruction. The original station had no basement, but this development would provide a range of services, including left luggage and toilets with access by stairs and lifts, the facilities being fully accessible. Plant rooms could also be housed in the basement.

It was now time to install the steelwork on the train shed's west side. This began on 15 December 2018 with the lifting of the 74-metre long truss in three parts that was placed by a 750-tonne crane – a night time effort when weather conditions were benign. By January 2019, the south flank of the train shed was prepared for the lift of the south truss. This time, a tandem lift involving two 500-tonne cranes that had gained access from West George Street, was also successfully accomplished. These trusses were crucial structural elements and the aim was to complete the remaining 1,400 tonnes

of steel structure by April 2019.

With this formidable task done, attention turned to the roofing. Above the concourse, with its new steel framework, the roof is a 'sandwich' of materials. This begins with a metal liner tray, followed by a vapour control layer, mineral wool insulation and then aluminium extrusions on top. The insulation reduces noise from 'rain drumming' and also condensation problems. The roof 'sandwich' narrows towards its edges to give a light appearance. For roofing over plant areas, concrete paving slabs were used.

For observers of the station's progress, the glazing of the West George Street side was continually intriguing. Here elevating platforms of the 'super cherry picker' variety were in action with the glaziers in abseil gear. With the design having a fully glazed wall, heat retention and ventilation issues had to be addressed. This

The steel truss for the office framework at Dundas Street was lifted on 15-16 December 2018. (Peter Devlin)

Crucial in design and construction were the supporting 'arms' where the new curtain walls met the heritage train shed as seen in July 2019.

South Flank West George Street

Top: *Constructing the south truss at the West George Street site in December 2018.*
Middle left: *An element for the south truss being moved after assembly.*
Middle right: *The 53m long south truss was in place early in January 2019.*
Above left: *The 'Pierce professionals' securing steelwork in February 2019.*
Above right: *'The new frontage or 'curtain wall' soon extends along the train shed.*
Left: *' By March 2019, the framework's relationship to the train shed is clear.*

involved extensive energy modelling by environmental engineers with the use of a computer simulation for the internal environment of the concourse. Both CO_2 levels and temperature were considered, the interior being typically warmer than outdoors. To help control the ambience in the concourse, motorised automatic opening lights (AOVs) are linked to a Building Management System (BMS) at the station. This provides power to open the windows when sensors are triggered by pre-determined thresholds for temperature or CO_2. Typically, the windows will remain closed to minimise the traffic noise from West George Street. To promote air movement, the opening lights are located at both high and low levels. However, the location of the glazed facade on one of Glasgow's 'canyon streets' means that surrounding buildings will give shade depending on the time of year. Further interest will arise from the reflections of the neighbouring buildings, especially of the Merchants' House.

From a historic perspective, sewer systems replaced Glasgow's burns with drains and pipes long ago. However, major works took place on the Dundas Street side when a strategic sewer had to be reconstructed. Water supply was also crucial and much attention was given to the positioning of water mains in the new works.

By the summer of 2019, work could begin on the platform extensions necessary to accommodate trains of eight coaches - only platform 7 being already long enough. The making of the extensions was timed to take place in two four-week phases – first in July for platforms 2 and 3, followed in September by platforms 4 and 5. The timing of such disruptive activity therefore avoided the Edinburgh Festival in August when trains are inevitably busier. A priority was to tackle essential services embedded in the platforms – notably piping with asbestos lagging – before work on the extensions to Platforms 2 to 5 could begin. The concourse was opened up in stages to reveal the temporary infill of polystyrene blocks that could now be removed. The work was complex - girders associated with the low level 'roof' were strengthened, drainage and service diversions made, and the OLE adjusted. Class 56 locomotives from COLAS Rail were at Queen Street to take out spoil and bring in supplies. The new buffer stops from Rawie are a far cry from the early station where mounds of earth were thought sufficient 'stops' at the ends of two of the platforms.

For many years, a crucial issue at Queen Street has been the need to allow for the possibility of trains over-running and colliding

The lifting of the 90 tonne south truss on 16-17 January 2019 required two 500 tonne cranes. (Balfour Beatty)

Overleaf: *The steel 'forest' at the 'blast strengthened' curtain walls was well advanced in May 2019.*

Top: *Roof works viewed in June 2019 when initial layers had been placed.*
Middle left: *Cladding and other materials were craned up from West George Street.*
Middle right: *A triangular space was constructed to accommodate air conditioning units.*
Above left: *A long reach crane from Horizon played a key role in the roof works.*
Above right: *Another safe landing of roof components in September 2019*
Left: *A plant room at roof level being fitted out in February 2020.*

By June 2019 the curtain wall frame and concourse extension on West George Street now stretched to Dundas Street.

101

For glazing , elevated platforms and cranes were in continuous use in July 2019.

Glazing

Top: *With steelwork for the curtain wall completed, glazing began in March 2019.*
Middle left: *A close up of a Henshaw team inserting glazing strips in July 2019.*
Middle right: *Teams at ground level later fed glazing panels up to the glaziers.*
Above left: *Inserting glazing panels was a 'hands on job'.*
Above right: *By autumn 2019, glazing, with temperature control, was close to completion*
Left: *A vacuum lifter tackles a glazing panel*

Platform Lengthening

Top: *Freightliner locomotives removed spoil from excavations at platforms 2, 3, 4 and 5 in the summer of 2019.*

Middle left: *For lengthening works, platform 1 on the west side was tackled first - as seen in May 2018 while in limited use.*

Middle right: *Story RRVs were working at platforms 2 and 3 in September 2018.*

Above left: *Platform ends show the strengthened girders above the Low Level lines.*

Above right: *Concourse excavation prepared for a 'frangible deck' in July 2019.*

Left: *Safe for passengers, a frangible deck is complete.*

Strengthening works above the Low Level lines in progress at Platforms 4 and 5 in October 2019.

Insulation & Cladding

Top left: *A long reach crane lifts components for wall insulation in October 2019.*

Top right: *A panel is slung to an installation team at Dundas Street.*

Middle left: *The team then secures the panel to the prepared surface.*

Middle right: *The Dundas Street side awaits stone cladding in December 2019.*

Above left: *Going high – stone cladding at Dundas Street in February 2020.*

Above right: *Inside, stone cladding in progress at the west concourse access.*

Left: *The ramp with its black granite 'splash zone' in West George Street.*

Behind the Scenes

Top: *The glazed curtain wall fronting the concourse in November 2019.*
Middle left: *The stair access from the former North Queen Street entrance.*
Middle right: *A Network Rail team views progress on the concourse*
Above left: *The commodious offices for ScotRail take shape on the west side in February 2020.*
Above right: *A lift shaft to the basement nears completion; there is disabled access to facilities.*
Left: *The new basement contains a range of services, such as left luggage and toilets.*

Passenger Access & Concourse

Top: *In May 2019, how the main access looked from Dundas Street.*
Middle left: *Passengers exiting the station towards Dundas Street..*
Middle right: *Access was always maintained to the two Low Level platforms.*
Above left: *A busy concourse at the Glasgow Fair in July 2019.*
Above right: *A line of ticket gates to serve the High Level platforms.*
Right: *A cast iron column now in a strategic position on the concourse.*

Going for Gold

Top: *Gold panels being installed on the underside of the roof in November 2019.*
Middle left: *Light shines on the enlarged concourse in October 2019*
Middle right: *An elevated platform lifting the gold panels to roof height.*
Left: *The panels were then transferred to the installation team.*
Above: *Gold louvres on the office windows at Dundas Street in March 2020.*

Above: *Gold panels gradually covered the concourse ceiling – a task done at night.*

Below: *The gold frame for the heritage train shed draws the eye when seen from George Square in December 2019.*

with the buffer stops or worse. It was known that there was an insufficient margin on the old concourse for passenger safety if such an event should happen. This has now been addressed with frangible decking being installed behind the buffer stops; it is a system that can fold like a 'concertina' in an emergency and thus absorb impact.

For the new station offices on the Dundas Street side, the cladding consists of composite Eurobond panels. These are formed from a sandwich with a layer of fire resistant mineral wool insulation between two layers of steel to provide a robust external wall; this often exceeds the levels of fire resistance and thermal insulation required by the current building regulations. To emphasise the civic role of the station and to underline the significance of its busy western entrance, the passage to the concourse is a lofty three-storey space – set at a dramatic angle but following the main desire lines that passengers will take. The architects chose to use a high quality stone for the external surfaces here; this also had to take account of the station's security requirements – there being a preference for robust lightweight laminated materials that would resist fragmentation.

The BDP decision was to specify a rain screen system using 'Stonelite', a propriatory laminated stone system. This bonds a thin layer of stone to a lightweight aluminium-backing panel. These weigh 95% less than solid 100mm stone but are capable of resisting sixty times more impact than the latter. The stone cladding is from China and comes from a limestone region near Guangdong. The material was formed in shallow seas 200 to 145 million years ago and is fossil rich, giving the panels many remarkable patterns. The light cream stone is complemented by black granite inserted at low levels around the new structures to give a finish that will be more resistant to splashes and grime from pavements and roads.

Meanwhile, finishing touches were being made to the frame around the great 'window' beside West George Street. Here gold anodised aluminium panels, again with an insulating sandwich, have been applied to set off the design and bring a touch of opulence to this Glasgow thoroughfare.

By January 2020, the Queen Street project was taking place largely indoors – being concentrated on the basement where tiling and plumbing, with electrical and mechanical tasks

This is how the main access from Dundas Street looked in February 2020 with its cheerful message

A view over the concourse for Project Manager Joe Mulvenna in August 2019.

Left: *The Dundas Street side has access to the Low Level platforms, the ScotRail offices are in the 'golden loft' and strong 'arms' support the historic train shed with its classical columns.*

Left: *The stairway on the east side, showing the entry from George Square and Queen Street (left), with access to the basement by stairs and lift from the concourse. (Multivista)*

such as the installation of lifts, was ongoing. Painters, joiners and electricians were busy with everyone now focussed on the completion by the spring of 2020. A similar pace was visible on the Dundas Street side where the offices were making rapid progress. A new ticket centre and a pretail facilities were also in preparation. Care has been taken where the new facade meets the train shed, the solution being 'supportive arms' linking the structures. The new customer information screens were in operation during February 2020. Meantime, it was possible to see the benefits for passengers of a concourse almost doubled in size from 960m² to 1,800m²

Left: *The new basement has both lift and stair access. (Joe Mulvenna)*

Right: *The facilities for passengers are both practical and stylish. (Joe Mulvenna)*

with new facilities in its basement of a high order.

To achieve such a worthwhile outcome, there have been many organisations and interests taking the project forward. Balfour Beatty PLC has had overall responsibility with their Senior Project Manager Barry Nicol taking a lead. Other key personnel guiding the project have been Network Rail's Route Delivery Director Kevin McClelland, Programme Manager Tom McPake and Project Manager Joe Mulvenna.

Principal sub-contractors

The principal sub-contractors have been:-
Dem-Master Ltd, Bathgate, for demolition works,
Lyndon Scaffolding Ltd, Glasgow, for scaffolding,
Roger Bullivant Ltd, Alloa, for piling,
J&D Pierce (contracts) Ltd, Glengarnock, for steelwork,
Curtis Moore Ltd, Hillington, Glasgow for cladding and roofing,
Charles Henshaw & Sons Ltd, Edinburgh, for glazing systems,
Story Contracting Ltd, Blantyre, for railway works, platform extensions and frangible decks.

Their teams have taken the project forward to its successful conclusion – a station transformed for the better, both for rail passengers and for the City of Glasgow.

Left: *Queen Street station's golden frame and railway identity logo are now clearly seen from George Square.*

Below: *By night, the new Queen Street frontage lights up West George Street making a glowing statement for railways.*

Top Left: *The glass curtain wall facing West George Street. (Balfour Beatty)*

Top right: *The new style of station architecture shows 'deconstructivist' influences. (Lesley Monroe)*

Below: *A night time view of the glowing facade and interiors at Glasgow Queen Street. (Multivista)*

Bottom left: *A close up of the main entrance from George Square with its security bollards. (Network Rail)*

Bottom right: *A restored cast iron column is one of several supporting the Victorian train shed. (Network Rail)*

Acknowledgements

The interest of many people and organisations has made this book possible. First in line is Balfour Beatty PLC; it was the enthusiasm of Barry Nicol, Balfour Beatty's Senior Project Manager at Queen Street station that prompted a start to be made on this book. There had been investigation of archives and plans in the context of the Edinburgh & Glasgow Railway as part of EGIP, the Edinburgh-Glasgow Improvement Programme for the railways of Central Scotland, and these enquiries revealed much about the history of the station. In fact, the extensive works at Queen Street station have been the final piece in the EGIP jigsaw.

Network Rail, the owners of the station, also took an interest in having a written record of the Queen Street project made, with Kevin McClelland, Route Delivery Director, and Tom McPake, Programme Manager, showing support. As the works progressed, Joe Mulvenna, Project Manager, assisted with a series of site visits that were invaluable. John McLaughlin also helped with these. Edward Dymock of BDP, who played a crucial role in the design of the station reconstruction, also gave insightful information, as did Douglas Lawson of Network Rail. The support of Abellio ScotRail has also been most welcome.

Excerpts from Queen Victoria's Journal in the Royal Archives at Windsor Castle have been used with the gracious permission of Her Majesty Queen Elizabeth.

Staff at the National Records of Scotland and the National Library of Scotland gave advice about finding documents and plans of relevance and they are thanked for allowing the reproduction of images.

Special thanks are due to Andrew Boyd of the North British Railway Study Group, who read the typescript and commented thereon. Members of that group are also thanked for information. John Yellowlees, ScotRail's Honorary Ambassador, has taken an interest in the project throughout and given help and encouragement.

Queen Street station was never a popular venue for photographers and images of its interior are scarce. A breakthrough came with the assistance of Susan Pacitti, Licensing Manager at Glasgow Museums and Resource Centre, where a set of images was discovered. These are reproduced with permission of 'CSG CIC Glasgow Museums and Libraries

Looking east across the concourse from the Dundas Street entrance. (Network Rail)

The Travel Shop that houses the ticket office machines. (Network Rail)

Collections'. Ordnance Survey map excerpts are reproduced under a 'Creative Commons Attribution: 4.0 International (CC-BY) Licence with permission of the National Library of Scotland'. The National Railway Museum, through the Science & Society Picture Library, and the Special Collections at the Library of the University of Glasgow, have both allowed the use of images. The assistance of staff at the Mitchell Library has been much appreciated. The Victorian web has also been useful. Drawings from 'Mr Punch's Railway Book', compiled by J A Hammerton, enhance early chapters.

Special thanks also go to Hamish Stevenson who has again made available his extensive collection of photographs relating to Queen Street station. The help of Douglas Blades, Geoff Corner, Ewan Crawford, Peter Devlin, Steven Duffy, David Hall, Richard Kirkman, Colin MacDonald, John McGregor, David Shirres, Michael Stewart and Peter Stubbs has also been most welcome. The North British Railway Study Group Journal has been a source of information and of images, some of which first appeared in historic issues of 'Railway Magazine'. The drawings of locomotives by Euan Cameron and of carriages by Allan G. Rodgers give an impression of what travel was like at Queen Street in its early days. Both are thanked for their generous assistance.

Professor Bruce Peter has helped with material on the British Rail years at Queen Street and assisted with the choice of photographs. John Peter has prepared the images for this book. Photographs without credits have been taken by the author and remain her copyright. Every effort has been made to trace the copyright holders of other images and apologies are offered to any who have been overlooked or found untraceable.